THE WHI[illegible] HORSE
and Other Sea Magic

For details of Target Books see end pages

THE WHITE SEA HORSE

and Other Sea Magic

HELEN CRESSWELL

Illustrations by Robin Jacques

Target Books is a division of Universal-Tandem Publishing Co., Ltd., 14 Gloucester Road, London SW7 4RD

First published in Great Britain in a collected edition by Chatto & Windus Ltd., 1972, as *The White Sea Horse and other Stories of the Sea*

First published in this edition by Universal-Tandem Publishing Co., Ltd., 1975

ISBN 0 426 10882 5

Printed in Great Britain by litho by The Anchor Press Ltd and bound by Wm Brendon & Son Ltd both of Tiptree, Essex

Contents

The White Sea Horse

For my Father
with love and appreciation

Contents

[illegible]

Once upon a time a [illegible] girl [illegible]
[illegible] Her home was a [illegible] wooden
houseboat that bobbed on the waters of a wide and
beautiful lake ringed by mountains. She lived with her
father, who was a fisherman. He went [illegible] in the grey
[illegible]

[illegible]

I

A Surprise from the Sea

Once upon a time a little girl called Molly Flower lived by the shore of a grey sea. Her home was a tubby wooden houseboat that bobbed on the waters of a wide and beautiful bay ringed by mountains. She lived with her father, who was a fisherman. He went to sea in the grey mist of dawn and came again in the thick white mists of evening. Or perhaps he spent the day on the beach mending or painting his boat, and Molly would help him, threading the nets or sewing the tattered sails of his fishing boat, the *Grey Gull*.

When her father was away Molly spent the days on the shore, poking in pools left by the tide, teasing crabs that hid under the black rotting wood of the jetty, and collecting shells. Sometimes she climbed the warm sandy steps that led up to the village of Piskerton and played till evening with the children who lived in the cottages.

Her newest friend was a boy called Peter who had brought a string of donkeys to give rides to the children. He was an orphan, and used to looking after himself. On warm nights he slung a hammock between the pillars of the pier, but when it was cold or wet he found shelter with a friendly fisherman.

One night Molly sat dangling her bare feet over the edge of the sea wall and waiting for the first glimpse of brown sails far away on the world's rim. A blue dusk was gathering. Behind her the yellow lamps of the cottages bloomed one by one, and the fisher folk stood on the steps in twos and threes talking softly or crooning songs as old as the sea itself.

The fishing boats came over the rim of the world; trim and sturdy they travelled the grey water. At last they knocked against the sea wall and the men leaped ashore, throwing ropes and heaving and splashing and shouting to one another. Their shadows were huge and swaying in the lantern-light, they seemed like giants, and they laughed and sang until the whole village sprang to life in the darkness.

The villagers crowded round to stare at the catch of fish. They lay in piles of silver on the cold quayside, plump and shining like ripe fruit. When everyone had admired the day's catch they drifted away to their homes, the men hungry and ready for their hot stew and a blazing fire.

That night Molly could see no sign of her father. She had seen his fishing boat, the *Grey Gull*, coming in with the fleet but she had not seen him among the other

fishermen, and now she was left all alone on the dark quayside.

She strained her eyes in the darkness, but all she could see was masts pointing skywards and the faint glow from the heaps of fish. She listened, but heard only the wet licking of waves on the sea wall and the clatter of feet on cobbled streets in the distance.

She shivered and drew the woollen shawl more closely round her shoulders.

'Perhaps he did not see me and has gone back to the *Tubby Boat*,' she thought. 'If I go home perhaps I shall find him there already.'

She was turning away when she heard her name being called. She recognized her father's voice, but could not tell where it was coming from.

'Father!' she called. 'Where are you?'

'I'm down here, in the boat. Can you give me a hand?'

She ran to where her father's boat was moored to a ring in the sea wall, and leaned over.

'Father, why are you still in the boat? I thought you had gone home.'

'I waited until everyone had gone home because I did not want a lot of noise and excitement. I have found something today, Molly, so strange and wonderful that I hardly know what it is myself.'

'What is it? What is it?' asked Molly excitedly, leaning over so far that she almost lost her balance.

'I shall be fishing you out if you don't stand still,' said Mr Flower, laughing. 'See, I'll pass it up to you. It's not very heavy, but hold it gently until I come.'

He stretched up his arms and Molly reached down and

felt something very soft and warm. She looked down but could not see what it was, only that it was white and was shining faintly even in the darkness. She stood alone on the windy quay prickling with excitement.

Her father clambered up beside her.

'Well?' he said. 'What do you make of that?'

'What is it, Father?' asked Molly. 'Do tell me. And where did you find it?'

'Wait until we are home,' he said.

He gently lifted the animal from Molly's arms, and taking her by the hand, strode off towards the other end of the bay. In the *Tubby Boat* there was a hot hungry smell of stew, the light from the fire stroked the walls and the shadows yawned and stretched like sleepy cats. Molly's father laid the animal on the patchwork rug before the fire. Molly knelt beside it, staring in wonder.

It was a tiny horse of purest white, so delicate that he seemed to be carved from ice. His hooves were of gold and they shone yellow in the firelight, and his ears pricked like petals, as though he were listening. His eyes were as clear and yellow as September moons.

'Father,' whispered Molly, 'isn't he beautiful? Where did you find him?'

'I drew him in with my nets. When I saw him lying there at the bottom of the boat I thought I was dreaming, I would have put him back in the sea but he seemed tired. His eyes were closed and he hardly seemed to breathe. When he has been fed and rested I shall be able to take him back next time the boats go out.'

'Oh, Father, can't we keep him? See how tiny and white he is! How can he live in the rough seas? Please let me keep him here!'

Her father laughed and shook his head.

'There are tinier creatures in the sea than this,' he said. 'I don't think he would be happy if we kept him here. But fetch him some milk, perhaps he is hungry.'

So Molly fetched a saucer of milk and the tiny horse began to drink. Then he struggled to his feet, wobbling a little on his long thin legs, and his moon-yellow eyes moving curiously and unwinkingly round the cabin. He took a few unsteady steps and then sank down again in front of the fire, his eyes drooping.

'He's tired still,' said Molly's father. 'Come away and let him sleep. It's past your bedtime, too.'

'But say I can keep the little sea horse,' begged Molly.

Her father smiled and shook his head again.

'I'm not making any promises,' he said.

And so Molly went to bed. But she lay awake for a long time on her bunk staring at the stars in the porthole and thinking of the white sea horse with his hooves of beaten gold.

2

Mr Winkle Steps In

Next morning the sea horse was as lively as a cricket. He twirled round the cabin on his spindly legs and his dandelion-puff mane spun round his head in a halo hiding his yellow eyes.

'He's lively enough to go back into the sea straight away,' said Mr Flower.

'Oh, please let me keep him just for one day,' begged Molly. 'I want to show him to Peter.'

'Very well,' agreed her father. 'Just for one day. But tomorrow I shall take him and put him back in the sea where he belongs.'

That day her father went with the other fishermen to a fishing town farther along the coast, to buy new nets and tackle ready for the winter.

When he had gone, Molly plaited a rope from seaweed and made it into a collar and lead. The sea horse stood quietly while she put it on and they jumped from the rockety *Tubby Boat* and set off for the village.

The sea horse kept tugging so that he could walk right at the very edge of the sea, picking his way delicately over the smooth bleached pebbles and dipping his buttercup hooves in the grey water as often as he could. The seagulls screeched with surprise, crabs poked their heads from under stones to stare and even the waves seemed startled, their white crests of hair sticking up on end.

Soon they were under the pier where the air was very green and cold and a strong wet smell of fish and seaweed came up from the sand. There was no sign of Peter, though in the distance Molly could see the donkeys racing on the level sands. Urchin and Rascal were in the lead as usual. Molly cupped her hands and called: 'Peter!'

A hollow echo ran between the arches and whispered right down to the very edge of the sea: 'Peter, Peter, Peter . . .'

She waited, and then she heard the reply: 'I'm here!'

'Here, here, here . . .' the echoes sighed.

She ran weaving through the pillars up the beach and saw Peter's tousled head sticking over the side of his hammock high among the beams and rafters of the pier.

'Hullo! Don't shout so loudly! I might have fallen out!'

'Get up, lazy!' said Molly. 'Why are you still in your hammock?'

'I didn't go to bed until midnight. The tide was in and

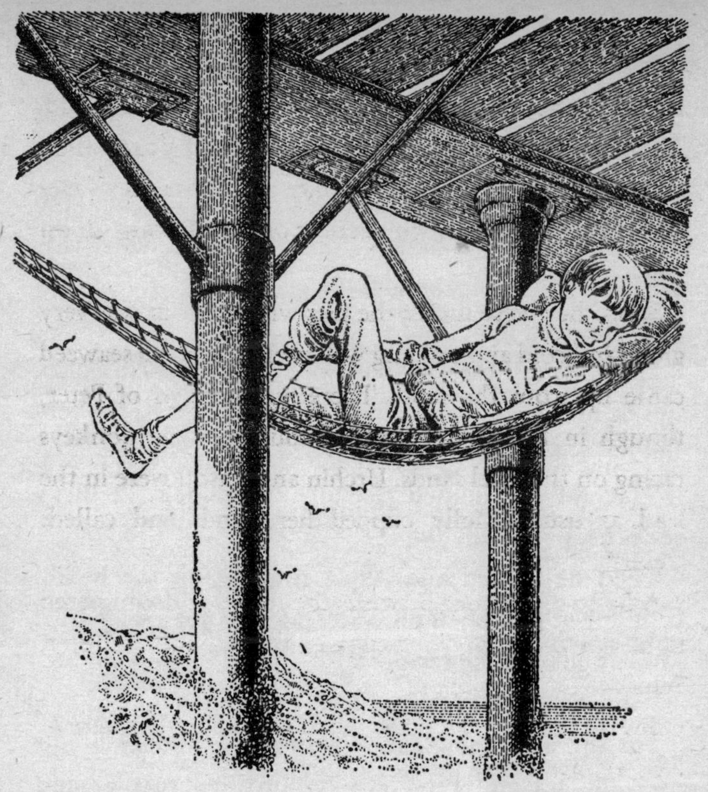

I had to wait until it went out before I could climb up.'

'Come down quickly, Peter, I want to show you something.'

'Here I come.'

He swung himself over the side of the hammock and clambered down the beams and pillars until he sprang nimbly to Molly's side. His eyes grew huge when he saw the sea horse.

'My goodness! Whatever's that? That's not a donkey!'

'Of course not. It's a sea horse. My father caught it in his nets last night.'

'A sea horse!' Peter shouted and jumped high into the air. 'A real live sea horse! Don't you know what that means? Luck! It's lucky to find a sea horse. It's lucky even to touch one. Quick, let me touch him!'

He grabbed at the little horse, who shied away in alarm, but he managed to touch its flyaway mane with the very tips of his fingers.

'Hurray!' he shouted gleefully. 'I touched the lucky sea horse!'

Then he turned and began running up the beach, shouting at the top of his voice: 'Molly's got a sea horse! Molly's got a lucky sea horse!'

'Stop, Peter, stop!' she called.

But the wind blew her voice sideways and away out over the sea and Peter ran on, growing smaller and smaller in the distance. She could see him running up the steps to the village and his voice was blown back to her, still shouting: 'Molly's got a sea horse! Come and touch the lucky sea horse!'

Molly gave up and stood for a few minutes panting.

'Oh dear,' she said. 'Now I suppose the whole village will want to see him.'

She began to walk back with the sea horse towards the

Tubby Boat across the bay. When they reached home they went down to the cabin, and Molly gave the horse a saucer of milk. As he was lapping it up she heard the sound of voices coming nearer, and she thought she heard her name being called. She went up on to the deck, and an amazing sight met her eyes.

Every single person in the village seemed to be there, crowding on the shingle and peering and craning his neck to catch a glimpse of the sea horse. At the very front was the village Mayor, Mr Winkle, who had put on his red robe and gold chain, but had bare feet and rolled-up trousers because he had been shrimping in the pools when Peter had brought the news. At his side stood Mr Bellow, the village Crier, with his big brass bell and three-cornered hat.

When the villagers saw Molly standing on the deck of the *Tubby Boat* they all stopped talking and for a moment it was so quiet that you could hear the water lapping on the sides of the boat. Everyone nudged everyone else, hoping that someone would pluck up courage to say the first word.

Molly stood waiting. She caught sight of Peter hiding right at the back and looking rather red and ashamed of himself. At last, Mr Winkle spoke.

'It has come to my notice,' he said, 'that you have a—er—er—sea horse in your possession.'

'Yes, I have,' Molly told him. 'But I brought him here because I don't want him to be frightened. If you want to see him you must come in ones and twos and not make so much noise.'

Mr Winkle cleared his throat.

'Mr Bellow, read the notice,' he commanded.

Mr Bellow then cleared *his* throat, took a deep breath and rang his bell noisily, shouting very loudly at the same time.

'Oyez! Oyez! It is hereby proclaimed by order of His Worship the Mayor that the white sea horse found in Piskerton Bay should be handed over to the Mayor, to be kept safely as the village mascot and to bring luck and good fortune to the people of Piskerton. Oyez! Oyez! Oyez!'

Someone in the crowd gave a feeble cheer and began to clap, and the next minute all the people were clapping and cheering and shouting.

'The sea horse! We want to see it! Bring out the sea horse!'

At that very moment the tiny white horse stepped up on to the deck of the *Tubby Boat* beside Molly and a little gasp of wonder ran through the crowd as they saw him standing there, his golden hooves flashing fire in the sunlight.

'Ah!' they breathed. 'Look! Isn't he beautiful?'

Then, before anyone could stop him, a little ragged boy in the crowd jumped forward and grabbed the lead of plaited seaweed and tugged the little horse away from Molly. She tried to stop him but it was too late.

The crowd of fisher folk flocked round him, admiring him and trying to touch his soft white coat. Soon they marched away in procession, led by Mr Winkle proudly holding the plaited seaweed, and leaving Molly all alone on the deck of the *Tubby Boat*.

3

The Bamboo Cage

When Molly's father came home that night and found that the sea horse had been taken away he was very angry.

'We shall see about that!' he said.

And as soon as he had eaten his stew and cleaned his rubber boots he went marching up to the village to see the Mayor.

When he reached the Mayor's house he rapped sharply on the brass knocker and waited, but there was no reply. The parrot which swung in a cage in the gusty porch shrieked: 'The Mayor's gone to the village hall!'

So off Mr Flower went up the narrow cobbled streets in search of him.

There was a crowd of people standing under the lamplight outside the village hall and they all seemed to be staring at something. Mr Flower pushed his way forward and saw there on the steps, his yellow eyes wide with terror, the little white sea horse.

Someone had made a cage for him of woven bamboo, and lying in front of it were little gifts of flowers and painted shells from people who hoped that the sea horse would bring them luck. The cage was not very big, so that anyone who wished could reach through the bars and touch him.

'How dare you!' boomed Mr Flower, in a deep angry voice.

Everyone turned in surprise to see who had spoken. He stood on the steps of the village hall and faced the crowd below him.

'How dare you come and take my sea horse and put him in a cage!' he said. 'And don't you see how cruel you are being? Look how frightened he is. You ought to be ashamed of yourselves!'

The people, who were really very kind at heart, hung their heads and shuffled their feet, and some of them began to murmur: 'Let the poor thing go. It's a shame!'

'No!' thundered another voice, even louder than Mr Flower's. It was the Mayor, who had come out of the village hall and was standing on the top of the steps frowning sternly.

'No!' repeated Mr Winkle, digging his thumbs deeply into his waistcoat pockets. 'I say that the animal shall stay here.'

'I beg your pardon,' said Mr Flower politely, because after all Mr. Winkle was the Mayor. 'I didn't know you were there.'

'Well, I am here,' said the Mayor. 'And as Mayor of Piskerton I am the one to decide whether or not to keep the sea horse. And my mind is made up. He shall stay.'

There was a short silence.

'Stay—he—shall,' repeated the Mayor with a long terrible pause between each word.

Mr Flower climbed a step higher so that he could look the Mayor in the eye.

'Why?' he asked.

A little gasp ran through the crowd. Here was excitement! Mr Flower of the *Tubby Boat* arguing with the Mayor himself in front of the whole village. They pressed closer eagerly.

'Why?' repeated Mr Winkle. 'I'll tell you why. Because that sea horse means good luck, that's why.'

He turned to the crowd.

'Is there anyone here who doesn't want good luck?' he asked.

'No!' they all roared in delight.

Mr Flower stood his ground.

'I want good luck as much as anyone,' he said, 'but I don't think it's right to keep that poor little creature shut up in a cage on the steps of the village hall. I would like to make a suggestion.'

'You may do so,' said Mr. Winkle graciously. 'I don't mind hearing other people's opinions as long as it is

quite clearly understood that what *I* say is what goes.'

'I suggest that the whole village should line up and one by one they could go by the cage and touch the sea horse. Then everyone will have good luck and we can let him go.'

Some of the people in the crowd called out 'Good idea!' and 'Yes, let him go!' and Mr Winkle frowned.

'Well?' said Mr Flower. 'What do you say, Mr Mayor?'

'I say this,' said Mr Winkle. 'I say that your idea is a good one, as far as it goes. As far as it goes. But there's another reason why I say that the sea horse should stay here. As you all know, in two weeks' time Piskerton will be holding a great fair and festival. And the King and Queen are coming to open it.

'Think,' said Mr Winkle, his cheeks growing pink with excitement at the thought, 'think of the honour it would be to be able to say to Their Majesties: "The people of Piskerton have captured a real live sea horse, and . . ."' here Mr Winkle paused dramatically, '". . . and they wish to present it to Your Majesties as a humble token of their loyalty and affection."'

'Hurrah!' shouted a little boy in the crowd.

'Hurrah! Bravo!' shouted everyone else.

'Go home, Mr Flower,' shouted the same little boy and then ducked behind a lamp-post, hoping he would be out of sight.

'What have you to say to that, Mr Flower?' enquired the Mayor grandly.

'It certainly would be a great honour,' agreed Mr Flower slowly. 'But I still don't like the idea of keeping the horse here in a cage. It isn't right.'

'Very well,' said Mr Winkle, who was in a good mood now that the crowd was on his side. 'We will build a high fence round the village green so that he can play on the grass. He will also be able to swim in the duck pond if he wishes. If he doesn't like ducks, then the ducks shall be moved. We will put seaweed in the pond to make it seem more like home. He shall have every comfort. I personally will inspect the village green every day to see that everything is to his liking. What do you say to that?'

'That is a very handsome offer, Your Worship,' said Mr Flower, 'and I agree to it. Mind, I don't say that I don't think the horse wouldn't be happier back in the sea, but if we are to make him a gift to Their Majesties then it's the best that can be done.'

'Then the matter is settled,' said the Mayor. 'I will have the fence built tomorrow.'

When they saw that the excitement was over the people began to clatter off down the windy streets to their homes and soon the square was deserted. The lamp-lighter came plodding by and snuffed out the lamp and all was quiet.

But the white sea horse in his bamboo cage stood for a

long time in the starlight straining his petal ears for the faint sound of the sea washing the pebbles and of seagulls crying in their sleep.

4

A Topsy Turvy Market

As the Mayor had promised, workmen came the very next day to put up a fence round the village green, and by evening the sea horse was in his new home. He stamped his golden hooves on the soft turf and whirled in and out of the pond in a halo of spray and everyone agreed that he looked very much happier.

The Mayor came to inspect him and declared that he looked very well and comfortable. He went so far as to say that on the whole he was probably better off than he had been in the sea, for there are no sharks in duck ponds.

In the evening Molly and Peter went to see him. He looked more strange and beautiful than ever against the green grass in the glow of the setting sun that turned his hooves to fire. He ran lightly to the fence when he saw Molly and his yellow eyes lit up. He stood for a few seconds while she stroked him and then he was off again, skimming over the grass in a fine mist of dew, never still, prancing and rearing and tossing his tiny head.

The next day was market day, when the people from

the neighbouring countryside came into Piskerton to buy and sell and enjoy a day by the sea.

'There will be plenty of children who want rides on the donkeys,' said Peter. 'Meet me under the pier at seven o'clock in the morning.'

But the first thing Molly heard when she woke the next morning was the rain beating steadily on the deck and pattering on the porthole as it slanted in from the sea. She looked out and saw that the sea was a dull grey and a little cold wind blew it up in ruffles.

By nine o'clock it still had not stopped raining so Molly put on her yellow oilskins and sou'wester and plodded through the wet sand to the village.

She found Peter in the stables where the donkeys were kept, polishing their harnesses. He was not in a very good mood and the donkeys themselves seemed restless and fidgety. They kept snorting and tossing their heads impatiently, wanting to be out in the open and racing down the sands instead of cooped in the warm steamy stable with the rain beating on the roof.

'Let's go to the market,' said Peter. 'Perhaps the rain will clear this afternoon.'

So they left the dim stables, and with the wind tugging at their oilskins they climbed the cobbled street with its blue puddles to the square in front of the village hall. The market was so noisy and crowded and full of colour that it was easy to forget the rain and grey skies. The stalls bulged with good things, from blue-shelled mussels to ballooning vegetable marrows, from cockles in vinegar to cornflowers from cottage gardens.

Peter and Molly climbed to the top step of the village hall and looked down on the bustling scene. In the distance they could see the village green and the tiny white speck that was the sea horse.

They saw something else, too, that made them blink with surprise.

Standing in a string peering over the top of the fence round the green were the donkeys.

As Molly and Peter watched they suddenly turned and started galloping up the main street to the village square.

'I must have left the stable door open!' gasped Peter. 'Quickly, Molly, we must stop them!'

But it was too late. The next minute the donkeys, with Urchin leading them, charged into the square. There was a tremendous crash and jangle as they knocked over a stall and left its owner with a saucepan over his head and all his pots and pans rolling merrily over the cobbles.

People screamed, children laughed and grabbed the oranges and apples that went skittling over the pavements and the donkeys brayed gleefully. Mr Bellow sat in the gutter with a string of onions round his neck, ringing his brass bell and shouting something.

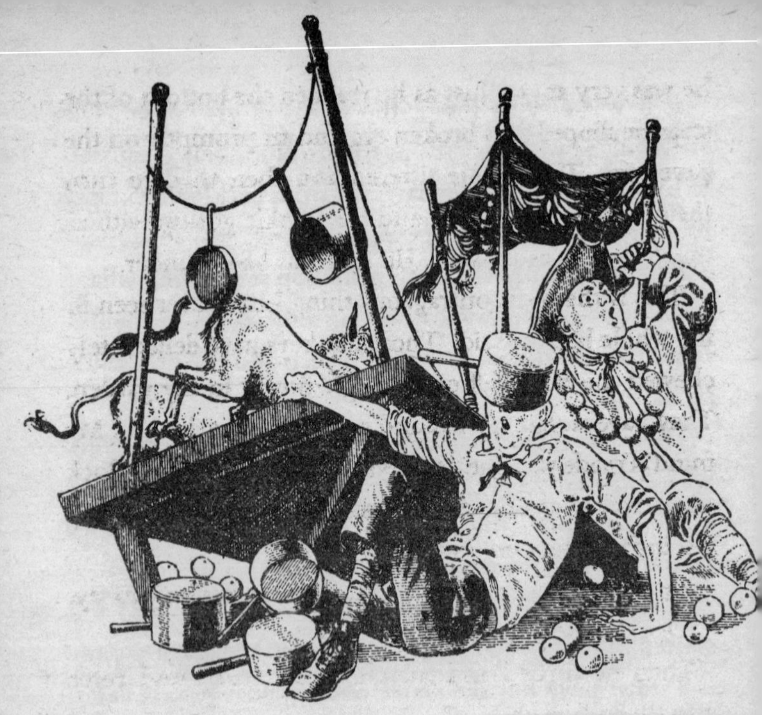

Mr Winkle came storming up the street, clutching his hat with one hand and waving a stick in the other.

'Who's chewed the heads off all the flowers in my garden?' he yelled. 'Who's eaten all my prize michaelmas daisies?'

The donkeys gathered themselves into a little knot and plunged down the street towards him. Urchin snatched off his hat as they galloped past and the next minute they had gone, leaving the market in ruins.

Mr Winkle stamped through the square and everyone stood aside in silence to let him pass. They could see that he was very angry. Just as he reached the bottom of the steps he slipped on a broken egg and sat promptly on the pavement. The people tittered and then tried to turn their titters into coughs, and Mr Winkle got up with as much dignity as possible. His face was like thunder.

'This is the most outrageous thing I have ever seen in my whole life,' he said. 'Those donkeys have deliberately chewed the heads off every single flower in my garden. They have stolen my hat and ruined the market. . . . My mind is made up. The donkeys must go. By seven o'clock tomorrow morning there must not be a single donkey left in Piskerton, or—or——'

He choked hard and tried to think of something to say.

'Or else!' he said at last.

Then he turned and marched past Molly and Peter into the village hall.

'We had better go and find the donkeys,' whispered Peter, 'before they do any more damage.'

They pushed their way through the tangle of fallen stalls and excited people and as they went they could hear people saying to one another: 'If this is the kind of good luck the sea horse has brought us we'd be better off if we let him go.'

Out at sea the Mayor's hat bobbed on the waves with several delighted seagulls perched on its brim. But that was something Mr Winkle would never know.

5

The Old Man of the Lighthouse

The next day the donkeys had gone, just as the Mayor had ordered. But the strange thing was, no one knew where they had gone. The villagers could talk of nothing else. The marks of the donkeys' hooves went right down the beach to the very edge of the sea, and then stopped! It was as if they had walked right into the very heart of the sea.

A meeting was held, and it was decided that Molly and Peter should row out and see the Old Man of the Lighthouse. He was the only person who might be able to solve the mystery.

The Old Man of the Lighthouse was very old and wise, and he had lived alone on the lighthouse rock for so long that he belonged to the sea as much as to the land. He understood the sea as if it were the palm of his own hand. Some people said that he went under the sea itself and knew all its secrets. If the donkeys had been stolen by the sea, then he would know.

The whole village trooped down to the harbour to see Molly and Peter off. A fisherman lent them his yellow painted rowing boat, for the rest of the fleet was out at sea that day. In the far distance they could see the lighthouse pointing like a warning finger into the restless sky. A strong wind was blowing from the sea and the waves were greeny-grey and choppy. The seagulls flocked together.

Willing hands carried the dinghy down to the water's edge and Molly and Peter climbed in.

'Goodbye, Molly. Goodbye, Peter,' cried the villagers. 'Come back safely!'

Molly and Peter took the oars and began to row until the villagers were only tiny specks on the horizon.

Seagulls whirled in circles on the wind in their wake, screaming uneasily. Once they were out of the shelter of the bay the sea became rougher and the wind fresher, whipping up the waves in green ringlets and blowing the salt spray on to their faces. All the time the pointing finger of the lighthouse loomed up larger. Soon they could see the white surf simmering round the sharp rocks on which the lighthouse stood.

'Look!' shouted Peter into the wind. 'Isn't that someone moving, out there on the rocks?'

'Yes,' shouted Molly, tasting the spray salt on her lips. 'That's the Old Man himself.'

In a few minutes the lighthouse was towering above them and Molly threw a rope over one of the iron stakes driven into the wall and pulled the boat in. A flight of rocky steps led up to the lighthouse and they clambered up them, thinking how icy cold they were from the endless washing by the sea.

At the top of the steps stood the Old Man of the Lighthouse to greet them.

His long grey hair and beard floated on the wind and his grey eyes glittered. A thousand suns had beaten his skin to copper and his eyes were very strange. He had gazed so long into the measureless distances of stars and seas that when he looked at Peter and Molly his eyes seemed to be focussed always on something beyond them, like those of a blind man. But his smile was kind.

'Good day,' he said. 'You have travelled a long way to see me. Have you come for my help?'

'Oh yes, please!' said Molly. 'We have come about Peter's donkeys. We think they have been taken away by the sea.'

The Old Man of the Lighthouse nodded his head slowly, looking from one to the other.

'Come inside,' he said.

He turned and led the way up the rock to the lighthouse. Hundreds of seagulls were perched on the rocks so thickly that they looked like patches of melting snow. There were other birds too, with strange curved beaks and mottled plumages of greys and browns. Their cries

were blown together by the wind into a kind of harsh music.

Once inside the lighthouse it was suddenly quiet and dim. The sea boomed beneath them with a distant roar. The furniture was very simple and was made of wood and the walls were lined with shelves of books, ships in bottles and rare shells. A flight of stone steps spiralled up to the lamp room and in the floor was a trapdoor with a huge iron ring.

'Tell me now about the donkeys,' said the Old Man.

So Molly told him the whole story, ending with how they had found the footmarks disappearing at the edge of the sea.

'We thought perhaps they had been stolen by the sea as a punishment for keeping the white sea horse prisoner,' she said.

The Old Man nodded.

'That is what has happened,' he told her. 'But don't be alarmed. The donkeys are safe and happy and will not be harmed.'

'But I want them back!' cried Peter. 'I don't want my donkeys to stay at the bottom of the sea. How can I get them back?'

'There is only one way,' replied the Old Man of the Lighthouse, rising and going over to a cupboard.

'What is it?' asked Peter.

'Have patience,' said the Old Man. 'You will see, you will see.'

He took three glasses from the cupboard and a flask of golden liquid and measured it out carefully. He gave a glass each to Molly and Peter and kept one for himself.

'Drink it,' he commanded.

So Molly and Peter sipped the golden liquid. They found it sweet and pleasant to taste and they drank the rest of it down greedily.

'Good,' said the Old Man when the glasses were empty. 'Now come with me.'

He went over to the trapdoor and pulled hard at the enormous iron ring. With a groan it swung open, revealing a flight of rocky steps. The Old Man lit a storm lantern and beckoned to the children to follow him.

They began to descend the steep rock steps. Their shadows swayed on the wet rock of the walls and the air was icy. Echoes shuttled back and forth around them and all the while the boom of the sea grew louder until at last they were almost deafened by it.

The Old Man stopped and they saw that they had reached the bottom and that a narrow creek ran at their feet. They could make out the outline of a boat. In the distance they could see the faint glow of daylight.

Wordlessly the Old Man got in and the children followed. With strong steady strokes he rowed the boat towards the opening and suddenly they were out of the cave and on the open sea, almost blinded by the brilliant sunlight.

6

The Enchanted Donkeys

They went through the collar of surf that encircled the lighthouse rocks into the calmer water beyond. The wind had dropped and the sun was shining and the sea was a smooth glassy green. Molly felt very strange and far away, almost lulled to sleep by the steady rhythm of the oars, and she thought drowsily that it must be something to do with the golden liquid they had drunk.

'Why did we drink it, I wonder?' she thought. 'And why has he brought us here?'

The Old Man stopped rowing and drew in the oars. He fixed his far-away eyes on Molly and Peter.

'Look down into the sea,' he said.

Dreamily Molly turned her head and looked over the side. Her gaze went down and down, right through the clear swaying depths to the very floor of the ocean. At her side she heard Peter gasp with delight and wonder.

The fish sailed by smoothly and slowly winding their quiet ways, barely stirring the seaweed as they passed. The sand of the sea bed was white and fine and scattered with a thousand wonders, so that Molly hardly knew

where to look first. She stared at the drifting shells and quicksilver shoals and groping sponges, and she did not even notice that the Old Man of the Lighthouse had picked up the oars and was rowing again.

The sea unrolled before them like a green carpet and time stood still. It seemed a hundred years before Molly heard Peter's voice, sounding a long way off as if he were at the bottom of a deep well, crying: 'Look! Look! There they are!'

The six donkeys lay fast asleep on the sea bed, their wild ears lying as flat and quiet as if they had been ironed down. Not a stir did they make, not a twitch of the nose, not a flick of the tail. Never had any donkeys been so still, and certainly never these donkeys.

'Urchin, wake up!' shouted Peter, leaning far out over the side of the boat. 'Rascal! Urchin! Wake up!'

But the dreaming donkeys made not the least stir. The spell of the sea was on them.

'You will never wake them by calling,' said the Old Man of the Lighthouse. 'Their sleep is too deep. They are enchanted.'

'Then how can I wake them up?' cried Peter in desperation.

'Only the white sea horse can do that,' replied the Old Man. 'So now you know what is to be done.'

'But the Mayor will never let him go!' cried Molly.

'He is going to give him to the King and Queen at the festival.'

'We must steal him away,' said Peter. 'I don't care for a thousand Mayors. Quickly, Molly, let's go back to the shore.'

Molly took a last look at the sleeping donkeys, like great furry mats on the ocean floor, and the boat sped smoothly away.

Still Molly gazed over the side, watching the strange life fathoms below, but gradually she found it more and more difficult to make out the white sand of the ocean bed. The water, that earlier had become as clear as glass, began to mist over again and now the fish were no more than shadowy shapes. Then at last all she could see was the surface of the water, calm and blue and deckled with little lines of foam. The golden wine they had drunk had lost its power.

As soon as they reached the lighthouse the Old Man led the way on to the rock where their own boat was moored. It was very hot now. The sun blazed down and there was not a breath of wind. He gazed up into the sky with his far-away eyes.

'There will be a storm,' he said. 'Goodbye, and good luck!'

They promised him that if they were successful in setting the sea horse frcc, they would send up a rocket to tell him the news. Then they scrambled back into the boat and pushed off. They rowed as hard as they could back to shore.

A great cheer went up as they drew the boat up on to the shingle and climbed out. Everyone crowded round them asking questions.

'What did the Old Man of the Lighthouse tell you?'

'Have you found out where the donkeys are?'

Peter held up his hand for silence and immediately everyone stopped talking.

'We have found out where the donkeys are,' he said. 'We saw them with our own eyes, asleep on the floor of the ocean. They have been enchanted, and the Old Man of the Lighthouse says that the only way we can set them free is to release the white sea horse. As you know, Mr Winkle is going to give the sea horse to the King and Queen tomorrow at the festival, so if we are going to set him free it must be done now!'

'Hurrah!' shouted the crowd. 'Set him free. Let's go and set him free.'

'Wait!' boomed a voice from the quayside, and turning round they saw Mr Winkle standing there.

'That sea horse belongs to the whole village,' said Mr Winkle. 'If anything is to be done the whole village must have a say in it. Nothing is to be done until the fishing fleet comes in.'

The crowd all muttered, and some of them said: 'He thinks there will be a storm and they won't get here in time.' But the fisherman who had lent his boat to Peter and Molly, and who could read the weather like a book, said: 'We agree, Your Worship. There is no harm in waiting until tonight when the boats come in.'

Mr Winkle gave a triumphant smile and turned away, and the crowd began to break up.

'I wonder why Mr Winkle looked so pleased with himself,' said Peter slowly. 'Do you think he is going to play a trick on us?'

'I think that he suspects there is going to be a storm and is hoping that the fleet will put into another harbour to shelter and not come home tonight. Then tomorrow it will be too late,' said Molly.

'It won't,' said Peter doggedly. 'Because if the fleet is not home by nightfall I shall go tonight and set the sea horse free myself!'

7

The Storm

That night the village was in a fever of excitement. There were all the preparations for the festival tomorrow to be completed, and then there was the suspense of waiting for the fleet to come in so that the sea horse could be set free. The people knew that if the storm broke before the fleet came in all would be lost.

A small boy was posted on the sea wall with a telescope and told to shout loudly as soon as he could sight sails on the horizon.

Mr Winkle walked round the village in his fine robes, making sure that all the preparations were properly completed, and all the time wearing that secret little smile.

As it began to grow dusk the huge black clouds rolled up in the distance and the air grew very still and quiet. Now that all the work was done the fisher people gathered in groups on the shingle to wait. They talked in low excited whispers, rather frightened by the breathless silence.

The seagulls were flying very low and uttering uneasy

cries and a strange yellow light flooded the harbour. Every moment the sky darkened and still there was no sign of the fleet. Then a shout shattered the silence.

'I see them! I see them!' yelled the small boy with the telescope. He danced on the sea wall in his excitement. His mother made him get down and they all strained their eyes for the first glimpse of sails. Slowly their shadowy shapes could be seen far out on the bay and at that moment there came the first distant rumble of thunder.

'Mr Winkle does not look so happy now,' whispered

Molly. Sure enough, the Mayor's face was as black as the sky itself. He began picking up stones and hurling them out as far as he could into the sea, and the people smiled and nudged one another. They enjoyed outwitting their own Mayor.

As the boats came nearer, the voices of the fishermen singing floated over the waves, and when at last the boats scrunched on the shingle everyone crowded round the men, all trying at the same time to explain what had happened.

Molly ran to her father and told him quickly all that had happened that day. He listened hard, and when she had finished he went and stood on the sea wall and called for silence. By now it was completely dark and they could only see his outline against the sky.

'People of Piskerton, do you wish to obey the voice of the Old Man of the Lighthouse?' he asked in a ringing voice.

'We do!' shouted the crowd.

'Good. I wanted the sea horse to be set free right from the very beginning,' he said. 'But I'm not the man to say "I told you so." We can all make mistakes. So what do you say we shake hands and be friends, Mr Winkle?'

The crowd cheered and Mr Winkle could do nothing else but go slowly forward and shake Mr Flower by the hand.

'And now,' cried Mr Flower, 'it's off to the village green!'

Everyone began to surge forward, but Mr Winkle stood at the top of the steps and spread out his arms to stop them. He was determined that he was going to give some orders for a change.

'Stand back,' he said. 'There is no need for everyone in the village to go rushing up to the green. I will go and fetch the sea horse while you stay here.'

'I don't trust him,' whispered Peter, and stepping forward he said politely: 'Don't you think it would be better, Your Worship, if Molly went? After all, it is her sea horse and he's used to her. He might be afraid of someone as grand as you.'

'Yes, let Molly go!' roared the crowd, who also suspected Mr Winkle of mischief.

'I'll get the rocket ready to fire while you're gone,' whispered Peter.

Molly climbed the stone steps and set off alone up the dark cobbled streets. As she went the first heavy drops of rain began to fall and there was a flash of lightning.

'Ah!' gasped the crowd on the beach, watching the lightning flicker over the sea. 'What a storm there's going to be!'

Molly hurried her steps until she came to the village green. Softly she unlocked the gate and stepped inside.

At that moment a great flash of lightning lit up the whole sky and she saw the white sea horse standing before her, his red-gold hooves and yellow eyes changed to purest silver, and his coat so dazzling that it seemed to throw off a strange luminous glow of its own. He trotted towards her on his spindle legs and she felt his nose nuzzling in the palm of her hand.

There was no need for the seaweed rope this time. Without a word she began to run back down the street, the rain slanting in her face and the sea horse galloping lightly at her side.

When they reached the harbour front she could see the crowd on the beach waiting for her, their pale faces and yellow oilskins gleaming in the darkness.

'Where's the horse!' they cried. 'We can't see him!'

As if in answer the lightning flashed and for a few seconds they saw the tiny horse poised on the sea wall, his hooves and eyes burning silver in the bluish light and his neck stretched eagerly as he sniffed again the salt of the sea. Then they were plunged into darkness again, and Molly heard a soft crunch as the little horse leapt down on to the shingle and raced towards the sea. Again and again the lightning flashed, and as the horse reached the sea's edge the waves seemed to yawn open and swallow him, and he was gone!

Almost in the same instant Peter lit the rocket, and

with a great roar it swept up into the sky and burst into a shower of orange arrows.

The sparks melted into the darkness and for a moment all was quiet. There was a lull in the storm and far out at the rim of the world the lamp of the lighthouse flashed.

Quietly the people turned and began to drift off to their homes, still seeing the little sea horse as he had stood poised on the sea wall with his eyes of silver and his straining neck.

8

The Spell Breaks

The day of the festival dawned. The sea was calm, the sky was a cloudless blue and everything was washed and rinsed fresh and shining by the rain of the night before.

By dawn the whole village was astir, the women scrubbing their doorsteps and preparing food, the men decorating their boats with flags and banners in honour of the King and Queen. The Mayor wandered about in a dream, rehearsing his speech to Their Majesties under his breath.

Mr Flower and Molly scrubbed the decks of the *Tubby Boat*, polished the brass fittings and hung her with buntings, and then slowly floated down the bay to the village to take part in the parade of boats. As they tied up, Molly saw Peter waving to her from the quayside and she ran to meet him.

'Where are the donkeys?' she cried. 'Are they in the stables?'

'They haven't come back yet,' said Peter. 'Oh, Molly, do you think they ever will?'

'Of course,' said Molly stoutly. 'The Old Man of the

Lighthouse promised. They'll come back, you'll see.'

'But I want them back today,' said Peter. 'All the children will want donkey rides today.'

'And what am I going to tell the King and Queen, that is what I should like to know,' interrupted a loud voice. It was Mr Winkle. 'I told them in my last letter that we had a surprise for them. Now I shall have to explain to them that after all we can't present them with a real live sea horse. But how can I tell them we had to let him go to save the donkeys, when there aren't any donkeys to show? I'm in a very difficult position because of those donkeys of yours.'

'Perhaps the donkeys will have come back by the time the royal procession starts,' suggested Molly, who could not help feeling a little sorry for the flustered Mr Winkle.

He snorted.

'Oh no, they won't,' he said. 'I wish I hadn't let the sea horse go. Fine gratitude he's shown for being set free. If I ever catch another sea horse I shall never let it go. Never!'

He stumped off to his house to give his parrot a last test on the poem he was to say.

The village band had begun to gather on the quay. Their brass instruments glittered in the sun and their faces were red with scrubbing. The last touches were put to the platform where the King and Queen were to sit,

overlooking the bay with its flock of gaily coloured boats. Even the seagulls looked whiter than usual.

At last all was ready and the royal coach was due to arrive. As it came rolling over the stone bridge into the village, drawn by four white horses, everyone began to cheer and shout and wave until the whole bay echoed.

Mr Winkle stepped proudly forward and greeted Their Majesties, and when he sat on the platform next to the Queen herself his face was in great danger of splitting with the enormous smile of pride it wore. He made a speech welcoming them to Piskerton and then the King made a speech saying how glad they were to be there and how beautiful the boats in the harbour looked. Then he said how much he and the Queen were looking forward to the 'very great surprise' which the Mayor had mentioned in his last letter.

At this the Mayor's face went crimson and the people held their breaths. Poor Mr Winkle!

Bravely he rose to his feet and began to tell the King how Mr Flower had caught a sea horse in his nets, and how he, Mr Winkle, had thought what a good idea it would be to present it to Their Majesties on the day of the festival.

'We thought it would bring you good luck,' he said miserably.

'How wonderful!' cried the Queen, clapping her hands. 'A real live sea horse! I have never seen one before. Where is it?'

'Back in the sea,' said Mr Winkle, taking a deep breath.

Then he told the rest of the story, and he was just finishing when suddenly someone shouted: 'Look! Look!'

Everyone whirled round and looked down towards the sea, and an astonishing sight met their eyes.

Coming up the beach towards them was the strangest procession they had ever seen, and at its head, miraculously, was the tiny white sea horse himself! His white coat shone in the sun, his hooves glittered red-gold and his eyes were clear and yellow as September moons. Proudly and delicately he stepped up the stony beach while everyone watched in awestruck silence.

Behind him, in a neat file, were the six donkeys. Their

wild ears flapped and their tails twitched. Round their necks they all wore rows and rows of shells, which clashed and jingled as they kept shaking the water from their rough coats.

'Look!' whispered Molly as the procession reached the platform and stopped in front of the King and Queen. 'They're carrying something in their mouths.'

Solemnly and one by one the donkeys approached the table and dropped something from their mouths. The King leaned over and looked curiously.

'They're oysters!' he said. He took a little knife from his pocket and prised one of them open.

'A pearl!' he cried. The crowd gasped and the King held up the pearl for them to see. It was twice the size of a pea and it gleamed softly in the sunlight.

Then the Mayor took out his penknife and opened the other five oysters, and, sure enough, each of them contained a large and beautiful pearl.

'What a splendid gift!' cried the Queen. 'I shall wear the pearls in my crown. And we have seen the lucky sea horse after all!'

But the little sea horse was already on his way back to the sea. No one tried to stop him this time as he cantered lightly over the salty pebbles and on to the flat shining sands, golden hooves blinding in the sun. The waves seemed to run forward to meet him and with a last graceful leap he sprang into the waters of the bay and disappeared in a shower of spray.

The King and Queen were delighted and praised the Mayor for his common sense in dealing with the matter, so that when the parrot forgot his poem and got all the lines mixed up it didn't really matter at all.

The festival was declared open and the rest of the day was spent making merry. Garlands of flowers floated on the waters of the bay. The donkeys were none the worse for their adventures and ran up and down the sands giving rides till the sun went down.

Then at last the music stopped and the golden coach rolled away over the grey stone bridge into the mountains and the stars came out. Mr Winkle snored peacefully, still wearing his proud smile, and the parrot swinging in his cage out in the gusty porch suddenly remembered his poem and said it to the moon.

Over the bay the moon shone in a shining path. Crab in his hole, gull in his nest, shrimp in his pool, all were asleep. If Molly had not been asleep in the rocking *Tubby Boat* she might have seen a hundred sea horses leap from the waves and dance and frolic on the silvery sands.

And just before dawn the cold grey tide rushed up the sands in one vast smooth sweep and then ebbed as silently back again, washing away their hoof marks as it went. The sea keeps its secrets well.

A Tide for the Captain

For my Mother with love

Contents

I

Tinker's Dip

There are still places left in the world where no highway runs and where no one ever passes through because the only road goes there and back again. In one of these places lived a boy called Peter and his grandfather, the Captain. He was called 'the Captain' because once he had been a sailor. Even now his voice boomed as if he were shouting over the thunder of waves. He still wore his old peaked cap and carried a telescope for spotting foxes or rare birds when he went the rounds of his farm.

'Not really a farm, my lad,' he told Peter once. 'Not these few pigs and hens and vegetable patches. But farm enough for you and me, and that's the main thing.'

Peter agreed. It was his task to feed the hens and collect the eggs, so fifty hens were enough for him. It was his job, too, to weed the vegetable beds. Quite often he felt that this was more than enough, but he was careful not to grumble.

'On a happy ship all hands heave to,' said the Captain. 'There's no room for laggards.'

He called his house *Sea View*, despite the fact that the

sea was nearly forty miles away, and certainly not in view.

'I see it every day of my life in my mind's eye,' he would say obstinately, 'so, as far as I'm concerned, it is *Sea View*.'

And when the wind was in the east he would go about with his face lifted, sniffing eagerly at the salt air blowing from the ocean. No one but the Captain could smell it, but on those days he was always restless and prowling. He fretted like a caged gull.

Their house stood in a clearing called Tinker's Dip, about a mile away from Luxton, the nearest village. There was no road to the village, not a real road with tar and signposts. There was only a path, a beaten track.

'It's you and me keep that path open, my lad,' the Captain often told Peter. 'It's our footsteps that keep it trod. If ever we were to go off for a month or two, why, when we came back, it would have gone. Vanished!'

Peter was excited by the thought of the wilderness about them, waiting to swallow that narrow, rutted track. Tinker's Dip was always in danger of being cut off from the whole world.

But the path was kept trodden by Peter going to and from school, and by Grandfather, who visited Luxton nearly every day. Once a week he drove Horatio, his pony, to the village, carrying his farm produce on a cart. But most of all, he went in to ring his beloved bells.

When the Captain had first come to live in Tinker's Dip, the belfry of Luxton church had been silent for more than twenty years. The first time the Captain had pulled on one of the rotting ropes, the bell had given one brief, cracked clang. Bats had panicked and the rooks had screamed and lifted off heavily to the safe elms. Dust and ragged nests fell on the Captain's upturned face. He coughed and sneezed and rubbed his watering eyes.

'It's a crime!' at last he thundered. 'A black and wicked crime! Eight bells there are up there. Eight bells rusting and choked with dust! Beautiful, booming bells, doomed to dumbness!'

He was very poetic on the subject of bells.

'Their clappers are chained by your idleness!' he roared to the amazed villagers. 'But I shall set them free. Upon my word I shall! Free!'

He pulled another rope and started another shower of twigs.

He was true to his word. One by one the eight bells were taken down and mended and tuned until their notes were round and true. He scraped away the grime of a quarter of a century and polished them until they gleamed like fruit in the grass. The Captain did most of the work in the churchyard among staring stone angels and astonished cherubs.

Nor was that all. When the bells were re-hung and their stout new ropes swung stiffly down the tower, the Captain found for every bell a ringer. Seven stout men he found, from the schoolteacher to the smith, and drilled them in the hours between tea and supper.

At first the villagers laughed and covered their ears as the bells jostled and missed and tripped over each other in the rocking belfry. Miss Herrick, who kept the village store and seven well-fed cats, complained that the din was frightening her pets.

'They run right up the curtains,' she said, 'and pull all the threads as they go. And there they hang, mewing their hearts out, till that dreadful clatter stops.'

But as summer passed, a new order came to the bells. By autumn their notes rang in a slow and measured peal. The ringers were learning their ropes. The winter dusks brought high, frosty skies where the notes dropped with echoes round their edges. The villagers would stand still in the street to listen, and slowly they came to confess that the bells were, as the Captain had promised, beautiful.

2

News

All this took place before Peter came to live with his grandfather, so he learned about it from the villagers and the Captain himself. The winter evenings were filled with his yarns, and often the fire would have shrunk to embers before they went to bed.

But in the spring and summer the Captain would often sit in the porch smoking his pipe till the last light faded and the gnats and moths rattled on the glass of the glowing oil lamps. It was then, perhaps, that he saw the sea in his mind's eye.

One May morning Peter set off to Luxton straight after breakfast to buy some twine at the village stores. He left the Captain making scarecrows for the vegetable patch.

'There's a letter for you,' said Miss Herrick, after she had found the twine and charged him a shilling. 'For your grandfather, that's to say. Captain Ham Hawkins.'

'That's him,' agreed Peter, and took the letter, with not the least inkling of what was in it or what excitement it was to bring to their lives.

At the Dip, the Captain had made one scarecrow and started on the second. The completed one had a hollowed-out-turnip face that looked somehow familiar.

'It's Mrs Larkin,' explained the Captain. He always modelled his scarecrows on people he knew. It made them more real, and the more real they were the more notice the birds took of them.

'Here's the twine, Grandfather,' said Peter. 'And here's a letter for you.'

The Captain stared at the envelope. He turned it over and rubbed it between his horny fingers.

'Well!' he said. 'Who's this from, then?'

'Open it,' suggested Peter.

The Captain nodded, tore open the envelope and read his letter.

'It's from Eb,' he said at length.

Peter at once knew who he meant. In every other yarn the Captain told, Eb had a leading part to play. He was almost as wise and bold and strong as the Captain himself.

'He's coming,' said the Captain. 'Here.'

But he did not sound pleased. Nor did he look it.

'Aren't you *pleased*?' asked Peter.

'I would be,' said the Captain, 'if he was coming by himself. But he's not. Not by a long way.'

'How many are coming, then?' asked Peter. 'And who?'

'There's him,' said the Captain, 'and there's her.' He consulted the letter again. 'Name of Polly.'

'His wife?' asked Peter.

'Nine years of age,' read the Captain, 'and the daughter of a drowned friend.'

'Coming to stay?' asked Peter, delighted.

'Listen, lad,' said the Captain. 'This is a long tale, and there's no need for all the ins and outs. The bare bones of the case is this. He comes, brings the girl, and goes. *She* stays.'

'When?'

'Tomorrow, I shouldn't be surprised,' said the Captain glumly. He stuffed the letter in his pocket, picked up his big penknife and glared at the turnip face of the second scarecrow. With a few swift turns of the blade he gave it a look sour enough to scare a vulture, let alone a few pigeons or tits. Peter started to edge off.

'Rot his timbers!' roared the Captain suddenly, pushing the scarecrow away from him. It lay on its back among the dandelions, glowering up at the innocent sky.

'Why don't you want her here?' asked Peter, puzzled.

'Why?' demanded the Captain. 'Because this here place is a ship, and run like a ship. And on a happy ship, all hands heave to.'

'But think, Grandfather,' said Peter slyly. 'It'll be an

extra pair of feet . . . to keep the track trodden, I mean. It is rather overgrown lately. I noticed it this morning.'

'Aye, that's true,' agreed the Captain. 'Not that a Polly's pair of feet's going to make a deal of difference.'

'It might,' said Peter. 'It might make all the difference between the path being half trodden and properly trodden.'

'Hmmm,' growled the Captain. 'I still don't see the need for a little Polly. Polly indeed! Sounds like a blessed bird!'

His annoyance was plain. When he chopped sticks the splinters flew like hail. He stirred the soup for dinner so gustily that it spat out and turned the fire into a nest of hissing tongues. He went round all day, clucking and crackling.

Peter only smiled to himself. By the time Polly came the Captain's annoyance would have wasted itself on sticks and stews. *She* would never know of it.

3

Polly and Eb

When Peter came across the Captain next morning he was standing with his legs wide apart and stiff. A hand kept creeping up to the back of his neck and scratching. Even from behind he was evidently worried.

It had been raining in the night and the clearing was even more than usually a-glitter and sunlit, because of the wetness, the flashing of waterdrops and soaking grass. To Peter, sniffing in the sharp air, it was a morning to shout and sing and even shiver in. Certainly worrying did not fit.

'Don't think about this Polly, Grandfather,' begged Peter. 'She'll turn out to be no trouble at all. I'll make sure she behaves herself and fits in.'

'Oh no, no,' said the Captain absently. He had forgotten all about her.

Peter followed his gaze to where the long grass lay combed back as if from a parting. He wondered if he were only imagining that the path this morning looked unusually blurred and overgrown.

'It's all this rain and sun bringing things on,' remarked

the Captain. 'I've never known things come on as fast as this. I swear the grass has growed two inches in the night.'

He stared accusingly at the long stalks, half bent back.

'If I was to stand here an hour or two,' he went on, 'I reckon I'd see that grass growing.'

'It does look rather overgrown,' agreed Peter. 'But cheer up, Grandfather. We've always managed to keep it trodden so far, haven't we?'

'Aye,' agreed the Captain. 'But mark my words, we shall want every pair of feet we can get this summer.'

'And here come some of them!' shouted Peter suddenly. He had caught the flash of colour under the green hail of the boughs, of scarlet, and dark seaman's-blue.

'Ahoy!' came a voice as deep and thunderous as the Captain's own.

'Ahoy!' the Captain shouted back, and next minute the two old seamen were face to face. They did not make much fuss. There were no slappings of backs and loud greetings. They simply stood and took each other in. Then, satisfied, they shook hands and cautiously began the business of getting to know each other again.

Eb was a giant, and Tinker's Dip shrank as he strode through it.

'Wait,' said the Captain. 'What about this Polly? The one you spoke of in your letter?'

'Here just a minute ago,' Eb murmured. 'Dancing along here, she was.'

'Wearing a red dress,' put in Peter.

'There!' cried Eb, delighted. 'There's a smart 'un you've got, Ham. The lad sighted her.'

'*I* sighted her,' said the Captain with dignity. 'And I see her now, what's more. Behind that oak.'

'Poll!' shouted Eb. 'You come on out and act civil. We know where you are, now, behind of that oak, so come along out.'

Polly stepped out immediately. She was very tiny, with long, dark hair hanging to her waist, and solemn-faced.

'Good morning, Captain Hawkins,' she said. 'Good morning, Peter. It is kind of you to let me come.'

Eb grinned and nodded his head approvingly.

'There!' he said. 'Proper little lady, ain't she?'

'Well, good morning to you,' said the Captain gravely.

'Hello, Polly,' said Peter.

'This is a pretty place,' she went on, looking about her. 'I think I may like it here. I like out of the way places off the beaten track.'

'This ain't off the beaten track,' said the Captain. 'There's a beaten track you've just come along, isn't there?'

'Oh, that!' she said. 'That wasn't really beaten. Half beaten.'

Peter was aghast. How could she have guessed that that was the very worst thing she could say?

'Now, Ham,' said Eb easily, 'you give me a look over this place of yours. When I'm finished at sea I think a farm might suit me as well.'

'Not really a farm, Eb,' said the Captain. The two old sea-dogs went off under the new curling leaves and left Peter and Polly to look at each other.

'I think you'll like it here,' said Peter, wanting to make her welcome. 'Grandfather is very kind. And you should hear him ring the bells.'

'Ring the bells?' said Polly.

So Peter told her all about the Captain's bells. He told her, too, about their work, and about the most important task of all—keeping the track trodden.

'You'll be another pair of feet, Polly,' he told her. 'Grandfather will be glad of it.'

She stared silently at him.

'This year everything is growing fast,' Peter went on. 'Think—every night while we sleep, the grass and the nettles and the brambles and ferns, they're all growing out there in the dark. And one morning—who knows?—one morning we may wake up and find the path—gone!'

In the distance Eb and the Captain laughed together. The Dip itself was very still. Only a frog croaked in the luxury of wet leaves.

'Goodness!' said Polly then, scornfully. 'Surely you don't believe that! Paths don't just disappear overnight!'

She ran off and he heard her laughter drifting over her shoulder. Peter made after her, thinking that his grandfather might very well have been right after all about this particular Polly.

4

Eb Goes, Polly Stays

'Till Midsummer Eve the lass'll be with you,' remarked Eb with his mouth full, nodding towards Polly.

'Oh—ay?' remarked the Captain, giving nothing away.

'I shall come for her then,' said Eb, after re-filling his mouth.

He wiped his plate shiny with a crust.

'Polly'll be a good girl while she's here,' he went on, his eyes combing the table in search of the pudding. 'Spoiled her a bit, I have.'

'She won't be spoiled here, Eb,' promised the Captain. He went to the oven and took out the baked jam roly-poly.

'She will, Ham,' said Eb, 'if she gets fed like this. Cooking's your strong point, Ham.'

'One of them, Eb. One of them,' said the Captain, neatly turning the pudding on to a dish.

'Yes, you've quite a few knacks, Ham,' said Eb pleasantly, pulling up his plate awash with custard. 'What about your Weather Telling? D'ye still go in for Weather Telling?'

'Have to,' said the Captain. 'On a farm you've got to be one ahead of the weather, same as at sea.'

'He's very good at it,' put in Peter. 'Everyone asks him. They don't even fix the day for the fair till they've asked Grandfather.'

'Will you teach me?' asked Polly in her clear voice.

'Teach?' said the Captain, startled. 'Aye, I'll teach you what *is* to be taught. But there's more to Weather Telling than can be taught.'

'I expect it's just common sense, really,' said Polly.

'Listen to her,' cried Eb delightedly. 'Her and her common sense! She's full of it, Ham, I tell you that!'

'Common sense,' said the Captain slowly, 'is all very well in its place. But there's some things it just don't enter into. And Weather Telling is one of them. And furthermore, this here place is on the very edge of nowhere—which makes a difference.'

No one spoke. Outside the birds whistled in the wet and primrose sunlight.

'I tell you what, though, Ham,' said Eb. 'It is quietish here, now you mention it. Not a deal for doing, either.'

'Quiet?' the Captain's voice grew thunderous again. 'Quiet? Not a deal for doing? I tell you, Eb, that even if there was no digging for doing and no bells for ringing, that there track'd keep me on the go from dawn to nightfall.'

'Where does it go to, Captain Hawkins?' asked Polly.

'It don't go anywhere,' said the Captain, 'except there and back.'

'Well, then,' said Polly sensibly, 'it doesn't really matter much, does it?'

'Yes, it does,' said the Captain. 'That beaten track's the road to the world from Tinker's Dip. The day that path gets swallowed by the moss and nettles, Peter and me is as cut off as if we was on a desert island.'

'But why should it?' asked Polly.

'No reason,' replied the Captain. 'Neither rhyme nor reason. Things happen.'

'That path certainly ain't none too clever,' said Eb cheerfully, 'but there's naught for worrying about. It's the time of year.'

'Could be,' said the Captain. 'But there's something I feel in my bones, along with the weather.'

Nobody spoke. There was nothing that anyone could say. Nobody else ever felt anything in their bones—not for certain, at any rate. They sat there in the golden-green light and the birds whistled.

'Don't feel much like walking after that dinner, Ham,' said Eb at last, 'but reckon I'd best be going along. We sail tomorrow.'

At the mention of sailing the Captain's eyes grew wistful. But he was a man content with his own lot, and he got up and helped Eb to shoulder his pack. They all watched him go, striding in his long black boots over the beaten track.

Then they went back in and were quiet for a while, as people usually are when farewells have just been said. The tiny parlour without Eb's huge presence was suddenly forlorn.

That night, the Captain sat for longer than usual on the porch; he was thinking of the old days. Staring into the dusk, he saw green seas and cockle-shelled shores where the gulls rode on the wind. The dewed grass of the clearing turned to surf, and he seemed to smell its salt.

5

The Weather Signs

Polly and Peter were soon friends and the Captain was in danger of spoiling his charge, despite his promise to Eb. He carved boats for her from pieces of bark and made up endless stories about mermaids.

It may have been living on the edge of nowhere that brought a change in Polly. When she first came, she did not believe in mermaids, Weather Telling, or anything else at all mysterious. Perhaps it was the green, growing magic in the Dip itself that was working on her. Whatever it was, it was slowly rubbing away her common sense and opening her eyes.

All the time the grass was growing in a long, inevitable surge. It spread and thickened and flamed with a fierce greenness. The Captain grew excited and lively. While Peter and Polly endlessly weeded the vegetable patches and beat the path to Luxton, he would spend hour after hour at his Weather Telling.

He had a small hut on the edge of the clearing. Here he did all his wood carving, put ships in bottles, and kept his telescopes and compasses and old sea trophies.

Although most of the credit for the Captain's Weather Telling went to his own bones, he had various aids and signs, too, most of which he had discovered for himself. There was a telescope for studying the stars and clouds, of course, and a good old-fashioned fir cone or two, as well as feathers that changed their colour with the weather. On the roof were three weather-vanes, a cock, an arrow and an iron galleon. When the wind blew they stirred and clanged and turned, doing a slow dance in perfect time.

The Captain had jugs for measuring the rain when it fell and special ferns and potted plants to tell him if it *would* fall. There were rods, barometers, bones and straws besides. The Captain would pore over them hour by hour, plotting the secret courses of the weather.

One morning Peter and Polly were weeding the vegetable patches as usual.

'It's too hot for this,' said Peter, standing up straight. 'I've never known it so hot.'

'It's like this every day,' agreed Polly, whose hair was sticking to her cheeks. 'Hot in the morning and wet in the afternoons. I don't know why the Captain needs to spend so much time in telling the weather. *I* could tell him what it will be. Anyone could.' She was altogether too full of common sense really to believe in the Captain's Weather Telling.

Just then the Captain came rushing towards them, his peaked cap jumping like a loose lid as he jogged over the rough ground, knee deep in grass.

'The signs!' he cried. 'The signs! Look! There's no rhyme nor reason in it. The feather says rain and the straw says sun. And it's the same with them all—all at cross purposes.'

Peter and Polly stared at the feather and the straw, which to them looked like any other feather or straw in the world. Polly in particular was not impressed.

'A feather and a straw!' she said scornfully. 'Whatever do *they* know about the weather?'

The Captain did not hear her.

'The world's gone crazy,' he said with certainty. 'There's the strangest things going off in this Dip. The needle on that old barometer of mine, it's swinging to and fro like a pendulum. From fair to foul and foul to fair in the bat of an eye!'

'What about your bones?' cried Peter with a flash of inspiration. 'What do your bones say, Grandfather?'

'My bones,' replied the Captain, 'are hardly in a fit state for standing at this minute, let alone Weather Telling. My bones don't tell me one thing. Not one thing. And no more do my signs.'

'Perhaps they've just gone wrong, and need repairing?' suggested Peter.

'Gone wrong!' the Captain groaned. 'Then what ails the weather-cocks, answer me that! Cock one way, arrow another, and galleon pointing heaven knows where! It's not in nature. My African ivy that turns towards the sun has climbed clear out of the window and wound itself round the chimney. I don't like it. Not one bit I don't.'

Nor did Peter and Polly. The green around them seemed to gather and darken for a moment in the silence that followed his words. Tinker's Dip was on the edge of nowhere.

Peter suddenly noticed a ladybird travelling across the knuckle of his hand, and seeing it made the world suddenly seem so harmless and familiar that his fears dropped away and he cried, 'Let's go and look! Come on, Polly. I want to see the weather-vanes turning all different ways.'

And she, too, brushed away the touch of magic and took the Captain's hand, saying, 'Yes, come and show us all your weather signs. And what if they are all mixed? Rain one minute, sun the next, no wonder they can't get it right!'

They had turned towards the hut when there was a shout.

'Ahoy there, Captain!'

They all jumped. The thought of magic in the Dip

had made them nervous. Even Polly. Even bold, common-sensical Polly.

It was Tall Henry Weaver from Luxton. He was one of the Captain's ringers—in fact, the best after the Captain himself.

'Ahoy, there!' called the Captain. 'What brings you here?'

'Nearly never got here at all,' said Tall Henry. 'That path of yours is going to rack and ruin, if you'll pardon my so saying. And I'm stung to death with nettles.'

Peter and Polly hurried off in search of dock leaves for

Tall Henry's poor blistered hands. The Captain and his visitor disappeared into the cottage.

'Oh dear,' said Polly. 'I hope he doesn't stop too long. What do you think, Peter? Have all the signs gone crazy, do you think?'

'They may have,' replied Peter seriously. 'We shall just have to wait and see what happens next.'

6

The Concert of Bells

When Tall Henry had gone, the Captain told Peter and Polly the purpose of his visit.

'It's the bells,' he told them. 'There's to be a special concert. And I'm to be in charge. Of course.'

'Of course,' agreed Peter.

'For the King and Queen, as a matter of fact,' said the Captain.

'For who?' cried Polly. 'Why? When?'

'Midsummer Day,' said the Captain. 'Their Majesties will be going through Luxton on their way to London. They're stopping to have a bite to eat with the Mayor, and asked if they could hear the bells. Just think of that! The King and Queen knowing about Luxton bells!'

'I'm not a bit surprised,' said Peter.

'There's to be a whole hour of ringing,' said the Captain with satisfaction. He thought of the long practices through the summer evenings. Night after night of them in the dim church tower with the rhythmic ropes and overlapping echoes. His horny hands twitched for the feel of his own thick knot.

'If the wind blows right,' he went on, 'or if there's no wind at all, it'll be heard in seven villages. Think of that! Those beautiful bells booming through seven parishes and three shires, and half the world with their ears cocked!'

Peter and Polly were overcome with the grandeur of it all.

'I'll go into Luxton tonight and hold a meeting,' said the Captain.

'There's a whole month yet, Grandfather,' said Peter.

'A month!' cried the Captain scornfully. 'What's four weeks to a belfry? Bells count time in centuries, not in days.'

He sat down at the table and began making lists and working out changes. He gnawed his pencil and scribbled until dinner was ready. Then he gnawed and scribbled until tea.

'Now I'm off,' he announced. 'When I get back, I should like a bit of cheese for my supper, Polly.'

It was only when he went out into the evening shadows of the Dip that he remembered his weather signs.

'Them signs!' he cried. 'I clean forgot! But there you are. Bells come before weather, and always will. You might just go along to the hut when I'm gone and have a look at that African ivy. I don't want my chimney choking. There's fires needed in there when the frosts come. And see what that cock and arrow are up to. The galleon needs a drop of oil, so it don't count so much.'

He tucked his music under his arm and went swishing off down the track. Peter and Polly looked after his broad back, flaked in sunlight. It was very quiet.

'Come along, Polly,' said Peter. 'To the hut!'

'To the magic weather signs!' said Polly gaily. 'Magic!'

They saw the weather-vanes first, and stopped stock-still.

'They *are* all pointing different ways,' said Peter in sudden awe.

'There isn't even any wind,' said Polly in a small voice. 'Not one single puff.'

Peter cleared his throat. 'I expect they need oiling,' he said loudly. 'Rusty old things.'

'Look, Peter,' whispered Polly, tugging at his arm. 'The African ivy!'

Its rounded leaves glinting like scales, the ivy came pouring through the window and went clambering up the log walls and on to the roof. There it coiled itself round the chimney, dark green and dragonish.

'It was only a little plant,' whispered Polly. 'Just a little plant in a pot, climbing up a stick.'

'What are you whispering for?' demanded Peter more loudly than ever. 'I'm going in. There are the rest of the signs to look at.'

N
E
W
S
N
E
W
S
E
W
S

He marched forward. They pushed open the door and went slowly in. In the silence was a long, slow ticking, like that of a clock that has nearly run down. Their eyes travelled to the wall opposite. There hung a massive black barometer, blank-faced as the moon, and its thin finger swung from side to side—fair to foul, foul to fair.

'It needs oiling, I expect,' said Peter in a loud voice.

On the long bench under the window lay the signs. Quills as long as your arm were glowing copper and amber. Straws stuck up like spikes or bent over. Rows of potted plants hunched over their secrets. Peter and Polly could make nothing at all of them, and were glad of it.

Just then, the bells began ringing. Peter and Polly left the hut and walked slowly back. Once Peter looked over his shoulder and thought that the ivy had left the chimney-pot behind and was starting to climb clear into the air.

Back in the clearing there were tasks to do; hens to be shooed to their roosts, pigs to be fed. Peter and Polly worked to the noise of bells. They stopped, started, jangled and stopped again. And always the same tune. When the Captain made beauty with his bells, it always started with the drilling.

7

The Tide

Twilight came and still the bells were ringing. Peter and Polly went and sat on the porch as the darkness drank the colours from the Dip.

In the belfry of Luxton church the bells at last fell silent. Peter and Polly could hear only the showering of leaves. Then the bells tumbled out a new tune: 'Polly put the kettle on, Polly put the kettle on!'

The notes came vaulting over the moon and Peter cried, 'There you are! He's finished! He won't be long now.' Polly obediently went indoors and set the kettle to simmer on the hob.

Beyond the Dip the surfing sound of poplars grew stronger and nearer. Though there was no wind, all the leaves were shushing and hissing.

'It sounds like the sea,' whispered Polly to Peter, who nodded. It sounded like waves running back down the shingle, sucking the tiny pebbles as they went.

All of a sudden, they knew that it was the sound of things growing. They could hear the scratching and stretching of roots under the soil, and the excited whispering of new grass, grown tall and tapering after five minutes under the moon.

Peter and Polly sat close and silent, feeling the green gathering and crowding about them. Then the Captain's voice came like muffled thunder, 'Ahoy, there!'—and they heard him wading and beating his way through the rising tide of green.

'Grandfather!' cried Peter, and they ran to meet him. 'What's happening?'

'I only just got through!' gasped the Captain, staggering towards the porch and his old rocking-chair. 'There's stuff out there growing an inch a minute!'

He sprawled in his chair and his quick seaman's eyes scanned the heaving Dip.

'We're awash, my lads,' he said. 'We're at sea!'

His voice was triumphant, almost as if this were something he had secretly hoped for and dreamed of, and at last it was coming true.

'What do you mean?' asked Peter. 'Cut off, do you mean?'

'Cut off,' said the Captain. 'There's an ocean lies between here and Luxton. We're clear over the edge of the world, and no mistake. Head over heels into nowhere.'

Neither Peter nor Polly had a word to say. They stood watching the deep, deepening sea, a sea without fish or crab or shell, a sea of waving weed and grass, shining under the greenish-silver light of the moon.

An astonished owl flew suddenly over the giant, bleached heads of the dandelions. He perched in a dog daisy that was all at once a tree, and hooted angrily.

'An owl in a daisy,' said Polly softly. And the last shred of her common sense went floating over the Dip for ever.

'I'll have my bread and cheese, I think,' said the Captain.

Peter and Polly were glad to go indoors, where the wooden furniture was safe and certain, where the clock ticked and the kettle sang. The tiny galley looked so familiar in the golden lamplight that they had to keep stealing looks through the window to remind themselves of the vast, dark tide that pushed restlessly about them. The Captain noisily chewed his supper and washed it down with great, sucking gulps from his enamelled mug, as if nothing at all had happened.

'The signs were right, after all,' said Peter.

'The signs are always right,' replied the Captain. 'Never known 'em wrong. African ivy still climbing?'

'At the rate it was going,' said Polly, 'I should think it has reached the moon by now.'

'Are we really at sea, Grandfather?' asked Peter. 'Won't we be able to get to Luxton in the morning?'

'If you was to ask me,' said the Captain, 'there'll be no way to Luxton tomorrow, nor the day after that, nor the day after that. *Nor* the day after that, for all we can tell.'

'What if there *never* is?' said Polly, dazed by the thought.

'Unlikely,' said the Captain. 'No, I don't reckon on that. And as for the concert, I'll carve a path to Luxton by Midsummer Day, or perish doing it.'

'And they'll send a rescue party from Luxton, won't they?' asked Polly. 'And cut a way through with scythes?'

'Bound to,' agreed the Captain. 'But not all that easy,' he added hastily. 'There's a mile of greenery between here and there, remember. There's dandelions grown to oaks, and grass to poplars. It'll be axes and choppers, not scythes, my lass.'

Outside the grasses washed and lapped, and the Captain's ears pricked at the old sea noises.

They went out into the porch and stood staring up at the moon half hidden by a buttercup.

'I think it's stopping,' whispered Polly. 'Don't you feel it?'

There was a sort of stillness, as if the earth had suddenly stopped turning.

That night the Captain slung his hammock in the porch to keep the long night watches. And Peter and Polly both heard the sea in their sleep, and thought they were dreaming.

8

Voyaging

When Peter opened his eyes next morning it was to a strange green light that washed and swayed over the white walls. He lay dazed for a moment in the slow green whirlpool of light. Then he remembered. Next minute he was up and shouting, 'Grandfather! Grandfather! Polly!'

He rushed out and saw that the Captain was up before him, standing in the porch as if it were the bridge of a ship, taking the lie of the land. His telescope was tucked under his arm and already he wore his seaman's cap.

'My track,' he said, 'is gone. Not a sign of it. I think it was over there.' He waved an arm in the direction of a clump of clover with heads as big as busbies.

In the early sun the magic in the Dip was stranger still than under the moon. Polly came out too and stared dumbly and stock-still up at the towering daisies. In the wooden coops the hens crooned softly in their own dusty sunlight. A blackbird whistled from the boughs of a celandine, and everything was impossible and yet just as it always had been.

The clearing in front of the cottage itself, once a close-cropped turf, patched with moss, was barely knee high. Beyond, the undergrowth of wild flower and weed was now a forest of strange new trees. Goose grass had grown tall and dainty as birch or willow, ragged robin threw out great ruffs of reddish blossom, and the flowers of the whortleberry were big as pitchers among the leathery leaves.

The Captain kept his telescope to his eye for a long time.

'The hut's still above water,' he announced. 'The African ivy's got wound round the weather-vanes, by the look of it. I shall have to get my signs started first thing.'

'It doesn't matter much what the weather does now,' said Peter.

'Weather always matters at sea,' replied the Captain. 'And we're as good as at sea.'

He was brisk and eager at the thought of voyaging on this green tide.

'And now we'd better take a look at the vegetables,' he said. 'Things round the back look a bit risky.'

They were met by a wall of green stems, grass like bamboo with tall plumy heads.

'Through the house,' ordered the Captain.

So they went back through the house and opened the

kitchen door. Their way was blocked by a giant nettle, its leaves wickedly juicy and full of sting. Beyond, Peter could see the feathery tops of the carrots waving like young firs, and cabbages like laurel bushes.

The Captain fetched his axe.

'Stand clear,' he said. He began to chop steadily at the woody stem. Soon he began to puff and wheeze, and still the wicked nettle stood. At last there was a loud crack, the nettle swayed uncertainly, toppled and fell, flattening the bamboo grass in its path.

'We still can't get by,' said Polly. 'We'd be stung to death. How shall we ever get to the vegetables?'

The Captain disappeared without a word, and Peter and Polly looked at each other with green-dazed eyes.

'What will he do?' asked Polly.

'I don't know,' replied Peter. 'But he'll do something. The Captain's used to this kind of thing. He was on the high seas for fifty years, and knows a few tricks.'

'Listen!' cried Polly. 'It's Horatio!'

The horse came trotting through the parlour between the stiff-backed chairs and carved dresser. The Captain's bewhiskered ancestors frowned down from the walls. Horatio came to a halt in the kitchen, and blinked mildly at the rows of saucepans, only ever so faintly surprised. After the doings of the night before, nothing seemed particularly astonishing to anyone.

The Captain put on a pair of leather gloves, took the stout rope that trailed from Horatio's bridle, and advanced towards the fallen nettle. Peter and Polly stood locked, watching.

When the rope was made fast the Captain stood back and gave the horse a quick slap.

'Go!' he roared.

Horatio moved obediently forward, stolidly trampling and ploughing into the foliage, up to his knees, then up to his ears in wildly waving leaves. The nettle trailed slowly after him. The way was clear. Beyond were the vegetables, enormous and safe.

The Captain let out a great yell of triumph, and the pigeons gloating in a nearby ragwort went scattering off into the sky.

Peter seized the thick fronds of a carrot and using both hands tugged for all he was worth. But the fronds were twice as tall as he, so Polly put her arms round Peter's waist, and she tugged too.

The great carrot burst out of the earth and sent them flying on to their backs. They lay among the long canes of felled grass and felt its sharpness pricking into their arms and legs.

They scrambled up and stared down at their prize. It was without doubt a most extravagant carrot. It was almost as big as Polly herself. It would fill fifty stew-pots.

It was a carrot beyond all carrots, and it lay there so impossible and comic under the daffodil sun, that all three of them started to rock with laughter. Tears watered from their eyes, and still laughing they went back indoors to cook the breakfast.

9

Life at Sea

After breakfast the Captain began to chart the day ahead. He and Peter, with Horatio to help, were to clear the path to the hut while Polly cooked the dinner and fed the animals.

'And tonight,' he said, 'we'll send up rockets.'

'Rockets?' cried Peter and Polly together.

'As soon as it gets dark,' nodded the Captain. 'To let them in Luxton know we're safe and in need of rescuing.'

All that morning he and Peter chopped their way towards the hut. It was very hot, and they were glad of the shade of the overhanging knotweed and campions. For the first time they knew the feeling of being close to the ground, like an ant or moss. They worked with the humming of tiny insects and the strong smell of earth and cold roots. Heady juices ran from the bruised stems, making them giddy—milk from the dandelion, sharp green sap from Jack-by-the-hedge.

At dinner-time they picnicked under a dragon root, whose purple-striped flowers hooded them from the sun. Afterwards, as they lay flat on their backs, there was a tremendous quiet, and they realised for the first time how the silence had grown with the green. They might have been under the sea itself. Even the air seemed to have thickened, and to lie deeply like water under the quiet boughs.

Then a pigeon came falling out of the blue, a carrier pigeon that circled the Dip and flew at last to the open doors of the loft above the stable.

They all lay, nibbling their grasses, and stirred not a foot. It was too hot. They were too sleepy.

'Carrier,' remarked the Captain at last. 'Best go and look.'

Peter sat up suddenly, pulling himself up by the stem of a dog daisy, whose petals rocked above him.

'From Luxton!' he cried. 'A message from Luxton!'

They all hurried out of the heat into the dim, cool, hay-smelling stable and up the wooden steps to the loft. Gently the Captain took the message from the pigeon's leg, while Polly filled the water bowl and sprinkled corn.

'From Luxton, right enough,' he announced. 'They say the track's gone their end, right from the edge of the village.'

'Are they going to rescue us?' asked Peter excitedly.

'Going to try,' nodded the Captain. 'Got three men on it every hour of daylight. They reckon it'll take a month.'

'A month!' cried Polly. 'That'll be Midsummer Day,

the day of the bellringing. And Eb is coming on Midsummer Eve.'

'We'll be clear by then,' said the Captain. 'I'll be on the end of my rope when the time comes, never fear. I know it in my bones.'

There was a silence. Only the straw ticked in the shadowy corners. Peter and Polly respected the Captain's bones.

'I'll send them word back,' the Captain said, 'and thank them for their trouble.'

So they went down and into the cottage, and the Captain wrote a message, which he read out to Peter and Polly.

'Tinker's Dip safe and above water——'

'If you put that, they'll think we've been flooded,' put in Peter.

'Flooded we have been,' replied the Captain. 'There's more ways of flooding than by water.' He went on: 'Well stocked and comfortable. All hands will lay to for clearing the track by Midsummer Eve. Keep the bells ringing and tell Gabriel to listen for the changes.'

Then he took out his worn, black, leather-covered log-book, and made an entry.

'That's all done and square,' he said with satisfaction, and back he went to the loft to send the pigeon off.

All through the hot afternoon they hacked and sawed until their faces dripped and their arms ached. Towards evening, they reached the hut.

On the roof, the cock, the arrow and the galleon were fettered by the dark green chains of ivy. Inside the hut it was almost dark, because the windows were shuttered with leaves. But as their eyes grew used to the dimness, they could see that everything was just as it had been. The long thin fingers of the barometer pointed to fair. The Captain inspected his straws and lovingly stroked his quills.

'All ship-shape,' he announced. 'I'll get up there on the roof and set the vanes going, and we shall be all set. You'd best get back to the Dip and start supper. I fancy a slice off that carrot.'

Peter and Polly set back towards the Dip. On either side the stalks reared. Branches of cow parsnip and groundsel met overhead, shutting out the sky, so that it was like walking through a long, echoless tunnel.

Before they reached the Dip they could hear the far-off blanketed boom of bells. The Luxton ringers were carrying on.

The Captain, sitting astride the roof among the coiling ivy, listened. At first a smile spread over his face; but as the bells rang on, and one tripped and another missed, his looks darkened.

'Too fast!' he cried impatiently. 'Gabriel, listen for the changes! Henry, hold back! Slower! Slower!'

But the ringers in Luxton were a mile and an ocean away, and for once the Captain's bells did not obey him.

When he returned to the Dip in the near darkness, he went straight in and fetched a rocket, without saying a word.

'They know we're safe now,' said Polly, who did not like fireworks. 'We sent the pigeon.'

The Captain did not seem to hear her. He lit the rocket and it rushed off with a blaze and bang that left them half blind, with their ears singing.

'Ah!' said the Captain with satisfaction, and he went in to eat his supper, feeling very much better.

10

Race Against Time

The first few days in the Dip quickly passed. There was the work to be done on the track. There was the strangeness of waking each morning to see the green underwater light. Polly collected the smaller flowers, the forget-me-not and periwinkle, and pressed them between the covers of the Captain's seaman's atlas, which was the only book big enough. For Peter there were flowers to be climbed like trees, and explorations of the forest. The Captain sang hoarsely as he worked in his hut or swung his axe. At night he sat late on the porch, his eyes feeding on the green and his nose twitching at the icy night smells, strong as the salt sea itself.

'There's dew in bucketfuls,' he would say with satisfaction.

Pigeons flew daily into the stable loft, and sometimes twice a day, carrying back the Captain's messages. Every evening he listened to the ringers rehearsing.

On some evenings, when the bells rang in order, the Captain was well pleased, and would sit nodding and basking with his eyes half shut. But if the bells missed or stumbled, he would mutter fiercely under his breath and rock his chair until the splinters flew. His fingers twitched for the feel of a rough rope and its old rhythms.

Then the weather changed, and for a whole week it rained, a long silvery rain like needles out of the navy sky. If Peter and the Captain went out to clear the track, they came back drenched and spluttering. The great flowers and leaves cupped the water in brimming pools, and as they toppled, it spilled and poured, soaking the workers to the skin.

But the Captain did not lose heart. He was a sailor and used to high seas. He went off to the hut through the spattering leaves in his yellow oilskin and spent hours there, poring over his signs, or carving, or making charts.

Then came the wind. Never had the Captain's signs had to work so hard. At first it was only a breeze that blew the hair from the dandelion trees, leaving only bleak white heads. It flew like spume.

'Blowed them raw, it has,' the Captain said. 'Not a whisker left.'

The Dip itself was sheltered and strangely calm. But, as the wind blew up, the vanes on the roof of the hut began to clank and stir and were soon wheeling in their old dances. The gale unpetalled the daisies till the ground was strewn with flotsam. The grass pitched and the pigeons from Luxton were blown sideways as they staggered towards the stable loft. At night, the sound of the bells was drowned by the roar, though the Captain sat straining his ears on the gusty porch.

At last the wind dropped. One morning they woke, and it was bright and quiet. There were only seven days left till Midsummer Eve, and their own end of the track had been cleared for only a hundred yards.

'We shan't get through in time,' said Peter.

But the Captain was staunch. 'We shall get through,' he said, though the tide was still deep and impassable between Tinker's Dip and Luxton. 'It's always risky,' said the Captain cheerfully, 'to live on the edge of nowhere.'

'You always knew in your bones that one day the track would disappear, didn't you, Grandfather?' asked Peter.

The Captain nodded slowly. 'I reckon I did,' he said. 'In my bones.' Then he went out to fell another dozen daisies before supper.

At last there was only one day left. Peter came running in before breakfast, shouting, 'I can hear them, I can hear them!'

They hurried out and stood listening. Beyond the heavy dripping of dew they could hear, very faintly, the sound of crashing and voices shouting.

The Captain threw up his arms and kicked out his

feet with joy. Cupping his hands to his mouth and drawing in a breath, he let out a vast, deafening, '*AHOY*', that sent the birds from nearby trees up into the air in a storm of feathers.

They listened. 'Ahoy!'—so faint that it was only their eagerness that caught it.

'They're coming!' cried Peter. He ran round the Dip cheering and waving his arms. The Captain scuttled indoors to fetch his telescope.

'Here, lad,' he said. 'Up that elm. Right up as far as you can. Into the crow's nest, and see if you can spy 'em.'

Peter swung himself on to the lowest springy branch, and as soon as he was on to the next one, Polly came after him. Nearly at the top he sat astride a branch and pushed aside the screen of leaves. He could see where the rescuers were without the telescope. His heart dropped. They were a quarter of a mile away, and tomorrow was Midsummer Eve. He could see the tops of the buttercups shaking, and thought he caught a glimpse of Tall Henry coming up the cleared part of the track.

'Let's go down,' he said, and heard Polly swinging her way to the ground.

'Well, my lad?' The Captain's eyes were bright and hopeful. 'Did you sight 'em?'

'Yes, Grandfather.'

The two looked at each other.

'But they're still a good way off, eh?' said the Captain.

'Yes,' said Peter. Then he burst out, 'Oh, Grandfather, they're a long way off. Quarter of a mile, or even more! They'll never get through, never!'

'No,' agreed the Captain. 'It don't seem too likely.' He seemed quite unperturbed. 'That track'll have to be cleared by something more than chopping.'

'How?' cried Polly.

'I don't know,' he said simply. 'But we're on the edge of nowhere, and that's a rum kind of place to be. Things happen. We'll have to wait and find out.'

11

Things Happen

On Midsummer Eve, all day long, Peter and the Captain worked at clearing the track. They knew in their hearts that it was no use, but at least it gave them the feeling that they were working for something. In the distance they could hear the voices of the rescuers, and every now and then they would exchange loud 'Ahoys'.

At six o'clock a pigeon came winging into the Dip. The message said simply, 'We shan't get through in time. Sorry, Captain. We shall have to ring the bells without you.'

The Captain's reply was equally brief. 'I shall be there.'

After that, they heard no more voices, and the sounds of felling stopped.

With the coming of evening, a new quiet gathered in the Dip. Peter and Polly found themselves talking in whispers, and even the whistling of the birds gradually died away.

After supper they sat on the porch. The full moon was already hanging, pale and perfect, above the beautiful, giant heads of flowers. There was magic in the Dip, so strong and near that now even Peter and Polly could feel it in their bones.

'I wish,' said Polly then, very softly, 'I wish the tide would turn.'

There was an enormous hush, as if the world had stopped in its tracks. Then, from the quiet sea of green, there came a faint whispering and stirring, a stretching and waking, as if it had been all the time asleep. The Captain stiffened, like a fox picking up a scent.

In a vast, slow ebb, the green began to go down, as if the earth were pulling it back. Soon, before their eyes, the track began to open. The daisies were like snails drawing in their horns. In Luxton the bells were ringing, and every moment they rang more clearly as the sky emptied. The birds which had been roosting in the weeds took to the air, crying, and in the midst of their clamour, Eb came striding into the Dip.

'Ahoy!' he shouted. Now the echoes woke about him. Polly ran to meet him and he swung her up on to his shoulder. He looked round him at the still shrinking grasses and the cloud of birds, and said, 'Never in all my born days, Ham. Never, in all my born days!'

And they knew exactly what he meant.

'There's supper on the table, Eb,' said the Captain. 'We were expecting you.'

They lit the lamps and sat down to bread and cheese and gooseberry pie. Eb, who was a man of few words, said no more about the miracle in the Dip, but chewed steadily, intent on his plate.

As they were finishing, they heard shouts and singing voices coming nearer up the track.

'What will that be?' said the Captain, puzzled.

Out they went, and saw in the dusk the waving flames of torches, and, lit by the moving yellow light, the astounded faces of the villagers of Luxton.

The whole village had come, or so it seemed as people jostled into the Dip. The seven ringers stepped forward and clapped the Captain on the back again and again. He stood there, dazed and proud, unable to think of a word to say.

The Mayor of Luxton himself was there, and he solemnly wrung the Captain's hand, then Peter's, then Polly's. He made a speech praising them, but, oddly enough, did not say how strange he thought the happenings in the Dip. Nor did anyone else. Where magic is concerned, there *is* nothing to be said.

'And tomorrow the bells will ring!' he ended triumphantly, and the Captain's back straightened. So they would, to seven parishes and three shires, those beautiful booming bells with their tongues of iron in the high belfry. The villagers cheered the roosting birds out of the trees for the second time that night, before turning to make their way back along the track to Luxton. The Captain watched them go.

'*That* track's getting a good start,' he remarked. 'All those feet.' But his eyes were very bright.

They sat on the porch, listening to the voices grow fainter and further away.

'I tell you what,' said the Captain at last. 'That tide that's just turned was of my own making.'

'Was it, Grandfather?' said Peter. 'What do you mean?'

'I've sat here many a night on my old chair,' said the Captain, 'pretending the sea's out there, and half thinking I can hear it. They sound like the sea, you know, all them leaves, when the wind's up.'

'I know,' said Polly. 'I hear it too.'

'And some nights,' the Captain went on, 'particularly after Eb here had been, I'd sit here, and I'd wish it *was* the sea. Just to go voyaging, that's all.'

They sat, thinking.

'And that's not all,' said Polly. 'When I wished tonight, the tide turned.'

A light, cold prickling ran from her neck and down her back, a thousand times more real and exciting than her common sense had ever seemed.

'I thought of that,' nodded the Captain. 'And you know what it means.'

'That there's a wish left!' said Peter, hardly daring to believe it. 'There are always three wishes, aren't there?'

'Always,' said the Captain.

'Quite apart from which, Ham,' put in Eb, 'I expect you feel it in your bones?'

'That as well, Eb,' agreed the Captain.

Eb chewed hard on his pipe for several minutes.

'If you was to give me a wish, Ham,' he said at length, 'I'll tell you what I'd fancy.'

'What?' cried Polly. 'Oh, what?'

'Well,' said Eb, 'I'd——'

'Stop!' cried Peter. 'Stop! Don't say it!'

Eb clapped his hand over his mouth aghast, and all four stared at each other, seeing what he had nearly done. Then they all began to laugh. Still laughing, they went inside and straight away forgot all about it, because the track was open and tomorrow the Captain's bells would ring, and at the moment no one needed wishes.

The Sea Piper

In memory of
the lost children of Aberfan
21st October 1966

Contents

I

The Garters

Davy and Fancy Garter were shrimpers born and bred. Even their daughter Harriet had been casting her net in pools since she was three years old. They lived close to the sea-shore in a ramshackle old wooden house that shivered and leaned with every wind and yet, for some reason, never blew right away. It was right on the edge of the jetty where every day a clockwork tide came smacking up and then went down again, leaving the bare, quiet, pool-strewn sand.

The people of Little Shrimpton were all shrimpers, if it came to that, and the day the shrimps disappeared seemed like the end of the world for them.

That day started like any other. Fancy got up first, as she always did, slamming the shutters back more to make sure everybody else woke up than for any other reason, for it was five o'clock and black as pitch outside.

Harriet, lying in her narrow trundle bed, could hear her grumbling and waited for the moment when the door would open and the golden shaft of lamplight would fall across the wall. One by one she heard the fam-

iliar morning noises, the rattle of the latch, the working of the old iron pump, the clatter of pots and pans. Then, in the intervals of silence, she heard the rain, pattering steadily on the roof and against the walls and windows of her tiny room.

Harriet decided at once to stay ashore. On fine days she would sometimes go with her father and help with the nets, but a day of dripping oilskins and wet, raw hands and no view through a curtain of rain was not to her taste at all.

The door opened and the knife of lamplight cut across the bed.

'Breakfast,' said Fancy, and was gone.

Obediently Harriet swung her legs out of bed and found her clothes in the half darkness. Her room led straight into the living room, and when she went out the table was already set and Davy was laying out his gear. Out through the scullery she went and into the tiny yard to the pump. The rain beat cold on her bare arms and face, and when she looked up there was not a sign of a star.

She worked the pump noisily to make sure that Fancy heard, gave her face and hands a quick splash and stumbled back inside. Thankfully she shut the door.

'*Wet* again,' remarked Fancy. 'I sometimes wonder if shrimps is worth all the trouble.'

This was a remark she often made and, as she obviously did not mean it, it was always ignored. Shrimps *were* worth the trouble, all the Garters knew that. Fancy, with an iron pot boiling and a basket of wicked-eyed shrimps on her knees ready to be 'got pink', knew it most of all.

'*I* don't mind a drop of rain,' said Davy, drawing up his chair. 'It'll be clear by eleven.'

'That's what you always say,' said Fancy. 'As if the *rain* knew what time it was!'

She set the steaming bowls of porridge on the table. As they breakfasted, slowly the grey dawn light filled the windows and the glow of the oil lamp began to pale. Then from the street outside came the tramping of feet on the cobbles and shouts as the fishermen greeted each other on the jetty.

Harriet, wiping the steamy panes, could see their figures outlined against the sky. Behind her Davy was drawing on his rubber leggings and in the scullery Fancy was slapping butter and cheese on bread and packing slab cake in Davy's basket.

'I shan't come out to wave you off,' said Harriet, as Davy straightened up.

'No. Don't you do that. You stop and give your mother a hand,' said Davy. He was almost invisible now under his oilskins, but Harriet could see his eyes, bright and excited under the drooping brim of his sou'wester, and for a moment almost envied him and wished she were going too.

'I'll be there for the weighing,' she promised.

That was the best moment of all, counting the day's catch on the twilit quay, sniffing the strong wet smell that came up from the dripping nets. It is the only time of the day that a real shrimper ever *can* smell shrimps.

Davy tucked his basket under his arm and was gone. Fancy and Harriet watched him from the door, splashing through the puddles towards the jetty where a full tide was impatiently tossing the boats.

'It'll be a good day,' said Fancy closing the door.

That is where she was wrong.

2

No Shrimps

Harriet and Fancy spent the morning in the outhouse on the other side of the yard where Fancy cleaned and boiled the shrimps. First there was yesterday's catch for boiling. This was the part that Fancy loved. To her, a shrimp was only really a shrimp when it *looked* like one—rosy and raw as a newly bathed baby, pink to its very whiskers. She crooned as she ladled them from pot to basket.

Afterwards they scoured the big iron pot and made neat stacks of the bowls and baskets that went to market. They had just finished when they heard wheels rattling over the cobbles and Fancy cried 'Horn!' and out they both ran.

It had stopped raining, a hot sun shone and the gulls were wheeling. Among their shrieks rang the note of a horn.

'Father was right,' said Harriet. 'Fine before eleven.'

Fancy did not hear. She was jostling her way through the throng that had gathered round Horn's cart. Every day he went to market at Lower Herring down the coast, taking the day's catch for the whole village. Now he was bringing back the empty baskets and, of course, the money.

Horn was a thin, surprised-looking man not unlike a shrimp himself. He had a shock of hair that seemed to stand up straight, beady eyes and very little chin. He was standing on his cart, slate in hand and money-bag to his elbow, calling off names and making a thorough-going business of it all. Each wife came forward as her name was called and collected her baskets, while Horn counted out the copper and silver and the rest craned and peered. When Fancy came back her face was very red. She opened her hand and Harriet saw a single gold piece. Only once or twice a year did gold come back from the market.

'Gold!' she cried.

Fancy nodded and thrust her hand deep in the pocket of her apron.

'That's for a new chimney when the time for fires comes,' she said with satisfaction. The chimney had been threatening to blow off for years, and had finally gone in a spring gale—gone to sea, they supposed, for there was not a trace of it next morning.

Fancy took the empty baskets back home and stacked them in high good humour.

'And another good day today,' she said. 'Another

gold piece, I shouldn't wonder. It'll be new laced boots for you, Harriet, if it comes off.'

This promise sent Harriet earlier than usual to her look-out post on the jetty that evening. She ran out along the black tarry beams of the breakwater to catch up with the tide, which was on its way out for the second time that day. It sucked and hissed on either side and every now and then managed a little extra slap to splash Harriet's skirt and stockings. She shaded her hand over her eyes, because the sails would come right out of the setting sun like moths round a candle.

She sighted them at last, gave a warning cry and ran back along the timbers to stand by the giant scales that stood ready for the weighing. All the wives of the village were out, and Horn himself came down, nodding and bowing as befits a man who hands out silver daily.

Soon the boats were inside the harbour wall and being made fast, and it seemed like any evening out of a thousand other evenings until the first man stepped ashore and without a backward look at his boat walked away. A second man followed, then another. Harriet stared. Davy himself climbed up now and Harriet pulled on Fancy's arm and whispered, 'What's the matter? Why doesn't he pull up the net?'

'Hush!' hissed Fancy.

The shrimpers all gathered together and advanced to

the enormous iron arms of the scales. The villagers watched. There they stood, fishermen on the one side of the scales, wives on the other. The crying of gulls stopped abruptly—or perhaps it had stopped long ago and nobody had noticed. They stood silent in the creeping dusk and Harriet could not think for the life of her what had happened, what was happening.

'Are we ready for the weighing, then?'

It was Horn, and if he had suddenly given a blast on his horn the effect could not have been greater. Harriet jumped.

'There'll be no weighing,' Davy said at last.

'What's that?' cried Horn. 'And why not?'

'There'll be no weighing,' said Davy,' because there's naught to *be* weighed.'

'What?' cried Horn. '*What?*'

A stir ran through the crowd. Davy held up his hand.

'We have sailed all day and cast our nets all day,' he said, 'and not a man of us has had any luck. There's no shrimps.'

'No shrimps!' The exclamation passed among the crowd in an excited hiss. Fancy's skirt jerked suddenly from Harriet's fingers and her wooden shoes clattered over the stones.

'But, Davy,' she cried, 'the shrimps are *swarming*! See what Horn has brought us from the market!'

She thrust out her hand and the gold gleamed in the cold twilight. Slowly Davy shook his head.

'That was yesterday, Fancy,' he said.

'Yesterday! The shrimps have been with us a hundred years! My father was a shrimper, and my grandfather, and my great-grandfather, and my—oh, anyhows, shrimps don't just make off in the night. There's sometimes more and there's sometimes less, that I don't deny, but as to there being none at all . . .!'

'There's none at all, Fancy,' repeated Davy.

They all stood there, nonplussed.

'So we'd best go home and eat our suppers and wait for the morning,' he said.

It was the only thing to do. The Garters led the way and they were soon sitting round the table in the lamplit room, where it seemed more impossible than ever that there should be no shrimps.

'You might as well say there's no birds,' said Fancy, pouring the gravy. 'You might as well say the sea's run dry!'

'The sea might as well have gone dry,' said Davy, 'if there's no shrimps there.'

'They'll be back tomorrow,' said Fancy.

Harriet wondered whether her mother thought the shrimps had just gone visiting. On the whole, though, she was taking it very well. She took out the gold piece again and smacked it on the table in front of Davy's plate.

'There goes the chimney,' she remarked. Then, brightening, 'Unless you catch twice the shrimps tomorrow, Davy. All today's and all tomorrow's! Think of it! Won't those nets be stuffed? And two gold pieces when Horn comes from the market. Chimney and laced boots all at one go. Fancy that!'

Fancy, in the right mood, could fancy anything.

After supper she made Davy drag an old net indoors.

'You might be needing it with all them shrimps,' she said.

The three of them sat round mending it, seated cross-legged on the rush matting, while Fancy talked about shrimping in her father's day, and her grandfather's, and her great-grandfather's.

'But never before a day without a single shrimp!' she cried happily. '*This*'ll be a day to remember, Davy!'

As the wick burned lower their spirits burned higher. When they went to bed it was to dream of shrimps in great, misty shoals, seas full of shrimps, all swimming down the cold tide towards the blossoming nets of Davy Garter. Fancy had won the day.

3

Davy Tries Again

Next morning Davy went off as usual with very little said about the happenings of the day before. The only difference was that today Harriet and Fancy went out with him to the jetty to lend a hand with the mended net.

'There'll be no need for it, Fancy,' he kept protesting. 'I've never needed more nets in my whole life.'

'You will today, ' said Fancy firmly, and the net went with him.

Harriet and Fancy stood and watched the sails dissolve into the mist. It was very still and only a little dawn breeze carried them down the tide.

'Perfect,' remarked Fancy. 'Absolutely perfect.'

For all that she was not in a very good mood that morning. There were no shrimps for boiling, and she prowled restlessly about the house, finding fault with everything.

'It's at times like this I could envy your Aunt Lavinia,' she told Harriet. Aunt Lavinia was not in fact Harriet's aunt at all, she was Fancy's, a fact which Fancy chose to

ignore. 'At least she's always got something to put her hand to. *Shells* don't go swimming off in the night.'

Aunt Lavinia lived at Lower Herring and made her living by gathering shells and turning them into all kinds of unlikely objects. Two penguins with mussel shells for wings stood on the dresser as a memento of her last visit, and Harriet herself had endless coloured cockle necklaces and painted shell-boxes. There were shells galore at Lower Herring, at Little Shrimpton hardly any.

Once the sun was fully up and sprinkling light on the salty flats, Harriet took her shrimping-net and went off. Fancy was not very good company that morning, and in any case Harriet herself felt restless and fidgety. Fancy's dreams of a vast shrimp harvest had seemed well enough the night before, but this morning they *were* only dreams and wanted putting to the test. Harriet wanted to see a shrimp with her own eyes. She felt as if it were a hundred years since she had last seen one.

Barefoot she picked her way over the stranded purple and green of the seaweed and with a thumping heart bent over the first pool. It was clear and shallow, only a flat puddle really, full of blue sky and with only a single tiny starfish to show that the tide had been. She hurried her steps down the beach towards the real pools, the deep ones, where a morning's patience with her net could fill a basket and earn her a few coppers of her own.

Time and again she drew her net through the water, in the end running from pool to pool until at last, breathless and nearly a mile away from home, she gave up. For a while she sat there, staring at the sea, half expecting it to look different now that the shrimps were gone.

Even then she half-heartedly trailed a few pools on the way home, in the hopes of capturing just an odd one, a lost one or a loiterer.

'If I could find just *one,*' she thought. 'Where there's one, there must be more.'

At home she told Fancy, who had washed all the curtains and was now scrubbing floors. She leaned back on her heels and stared.

'*That's* nothing!' she said at last.

'But not one, Mother, not a single one!' cried Harriet.

'That's one tide,' said Fancy. 'That's yesterday's tide that left them pools. Your father's gone out on a new tide. Those bits of pools down there don't mean a thing, that I *am* sure of.'

Harriet at once saw the truth of this. She put her shrimping-net away and began to wonder what was for dinner. Even so, for the rest of the day she kept glancing out over the puddled sands and was grateful when at last the tide turned and began to swallow them, one by one.

The whole village turned out that night. Long before the fleet was sighted they were out on the jetty, filled with the promise of certain excitement. Shrimps or no shrimps, excitement there must be.

When at last the boats did come in from the cold sea to the warm pocket of air within the harbour wall, it was like last night all over again, except that this time there was no need of questions. Even Horn had nothing to say.

Families drifted off home, one by one. The Garters themselves went in and shut the door and sat down to supper in silence. No one felt very much like eating. Fancy had been so sure of nets filled to bursting that she had made a special treat, a decorated cake such as she usually made only for a party. Now they sat and looked at it dolefully, hoping they would find the heart to try a slice when the time came.

'None at all, Davy?' Fancy asked at last.

'None at all.'

'There could be *three* times as many tomorrow,' she suggested, though without much enthusiasm.

Davy shook his head.

'They've gone. Clean gone.'

'Why have they gone, Father?' asked Harriet.

'That I don't know,' he replied.

'There's no reading the mind of a shrimp,' remarked Fancy, and the others nodded their heads in agreement. That was certainly true.

'Will you try again tomorrow?' asked Fancy then.

'What else is there to do?' said Davy. 'Try and try and try again—that's all there is to do.'

Fancy collected the dishes and cut into the cake.

'Drat them shrimps!' she burst out then. 'Ruination little things! And you'd think butter wouldn't melt in their mouths to see them come out of the pot. All our lives we've spent on shrimps, and this is how they serve us!'

She served out three enormous slices of cake that the knife had cut while carried away by her feelings. Stolidly the three Garters munched their way through it, as if it were a point of honour that none should be left—and another victory for the shrimps if any were.

Tonight there was no net to mend, and Fancy's fancies ran to gloom.

'We've got a bit put by,' she said, 'but when that's gone, we're ruined.'

'Now then, Fancy,' said Davy, 'don't get black.'

'I feel black,' she said. 'Black, black, black! What are we to do if they don't come back? We shall all end up gluing shells like Aunt Lavinia, I know we shall!'

'Except there aren't no shells,' Davy reminded her.

'I don't care if there are or not!' cried Fancy. 'I ain't spending my life gluing shells and stringing cockles. I was brought up to shrimps, and proud of it, and a shrimper I'll stay!'

'Why then, Fancy, so were all of us,' said Davy. 'And we shall just have to sit quiet and wait what the tide brings us. And perhaps we shan't have to wait so long, after all.'

Now it was Davy's turn to be wrong.

4

Down the Coast

Next day the fleet went bravely out to sea again, and the next. Each night the villagers, after a long empty day with no boiling, no Horn with his silver from Lower Herring, waited on the jetty. Each night they read the news on the faces of the shrimpers as soon as they sailed within the harbour wall.

Two weeks after the shrimps disappeared they held a meeting. The shrimpers came home early that day and went to put on their best clothes first, feeling that the occasion demanded it. Scrubbed, damp-whiskered and best-booted they gathered by the scales. The tide was right in, as if curiosity had got the better of it, and it nudged close up, determined to hear every word. Harriet herself kept glancing nervously at it, half wondering if it were eavesdropping, so unusually quiet it was, licking softly on the stony wall.

Davy had been chosen to speak first and what he had to say was very simple. They must all wait.

'We must all wait on the tide,' he said. 'It has served us well all our lives and is the only luck we have.'

Harriet looked at the calm sea glinting in the evening sunlight, and found it hard to suspect it of treachery. Her father must be right. But it was clear that many of the villagers disagreed, Horn most of all.

'I say down with shrimps!' he cried. 'There's plenty of other fish in the sea, I say!'

A murmur of agreement ran through the crowd.

'There's only shrimps in these parts,' said Davy. 'Was only shrimps, I mean.'

'Then,' said Horn, 'we must go where there is fish, real fish. I've never thought shrimps was real fish at all come to that.'

There was booing then, and cries of 'Shame!' The people of Little Shrimpton were proud of their calling and rallied to its defence. Horn held up his hand. His pinkness completed his resemblance to a shrimp.

'Very well,' he said, ' I will say no more. But I say this. There's been no silver brought to this town for two weeks and more. Five children I have at home to be fed and clothed. Where the silver is, I must go. If there's no silver here—then I shall go!'

There was silence. Horn had spoken the words that many a man in the crowd was thinking.

'Down the coast!' cried Horn. 'That's where the silver is! Silver mackerel and silver herring. There's *nets* full of silver down the coast!'

'Yes, down the coast!' cried the people, fired by the vision of bursting nets and showers of silver. 'Down the coast!'

Davy held up his hand for silence and tried to shout above the din, but in vain. Talking excitedly the villagers gathered in groups and made their plans. This man had a horse and cart, this a wagon. They would shut up their houses, take their belongings and go. The Garters, horrified, stared at each other.

'Come along, Fancy and Harriet,' said Davy. 'Home.'

They went in and shut the door. Fancy even banged the shutters to, to muffle the noise and excitement from the quay. They all sat down.

'So it's come to that, has it?' said Fancy. 'Down the coast, is it!'

'Not for us, Fancy,' said Davy.

'Shrimps isn't real fish, indeed!' cried Fancy. 'And what does Horn know about fish, pray?'

'Are there really other fish down the coast, Mother?' asked Harriet.

'I don't hold with other fish,' said Fancy with finality. 'I'm a shrimper.'

Davy and Harriet may not have found it as easy to keep saying it as Fancy did, but they felt exactly the same. There was really nothing more to be said.

Next morning the whole village was astir. Doors

stood wide and furniture and bedding was piled in the streets. Wagons were loaded high with chairs and tables, mattresses and cooking-pots.

'Even the pictures off the walls!' said Fancy in disgust.

The Garters watched all day from their windows. At noon Horn's family rolled by, with four of the children riding on top of a kitchen table, and the baby in a shrimp-basket.

'First off a sinking ship!' said Fancy scornfully. 'Shrimps isn't real fish, indeed!'

It seemed unlikely that she would ever forgive him this.

As the day wore on, more and more carts passed by the window. At the house opposite Samuel Stone began

to nail the shutters down—bang, bang, bang—till Fancy covered her ears with her hands and Harriet felt her head begin to ache.

All through the next day the work went on. The men saw their families safely off in the wagons, then took to the water in their boats and made off down the coast. Some of them came in to shake hands and make their farewells, and seeing their downcast eyes Harriet could not find it in her heart to blame them. They did not want to go, any more than the Garters did. They were simply less obstinate.

By the evening of the third day the village was deserted. The last cart rolled past the windows and disappeared into the gathering dusk. Then there was silence. The three Garters opened the door and ventured out. There were no lamps behind the windows, no sails to watch for, no eager women on the jetty. Even the tide was out.

'It's quiet,' suggested Davy at last.

'Quietish,' agreed Fancy.

A last gull called and their eyes followed the white shape into the smudging gloom. Now it seemed they had the whole world to themselves.

'I've just had a fancy!' cried Fancy suddenly, and the others started.

She began to laugh, pushing at her wispy hair with her hands as she always did when she was excited.

'Fancy if you was to go out tomorrow all by yourself, Davy, and if those shrimps was to have come *back*!' Her hands left her hair and flew clear into the air at the thought. 'Fancy if they was to be *there*, thick as noodles in a broth! Oh, Davy, fancy!'

Harriet and Davy stood there quietly, trying hard to fancy it. Slowly Fancy's laughter died away.

'Oh, well,' she said. 'Supper, then. Toasted cheese. That I am sure of. Drat shrimps!'

The Garters went inside and shut the door. All the doors in Little Shrimpton were shut now.

5

A New Plan

A new way of life began for the Garters.

'We've got to learn to live to ourselves,' said Fancy. 'And that'll mean work, all round.'

In the past a cart had come from Lower Herring each week with supplies for the village, with extra dainties and fruit and vegetables.

'And now we shall have to grow our own,' said Fancy.

There was a patch of thin, poor soil behind the house and Davy dug it as deep as he was able and sowed potatoes, carrots and beans. The Garters borrowed a cart from a nearby farmer and went into Lower Herring. There they bought sacks of flour, oil for the lamp, and a big salted ham to hang from the ceiling.

'What we really want,' said Fancy thoughtfully, 'is a cow.'

'No room,' said Davy, thinking of his newly planted garden.

'Village green,' said Fancy.

So a cow they bought, and half a dozen hens, which were to be Harriet's. They trundled home with their laden wagon, feeling like real farmers, singing songs and waving switches they had cut from the hedge.

Only when they drove into the shuttered village, when the wheels stopped rolling and the silence crept up on them again, did their spirits sink. To be sure, the tide flapped idly under the jetty and the gulls wheeled and screamed under the low cliffs just as they always had, but the people were missing, and they had left a silence that all the sea noises in the world could not hide.

They sat there blankly.

'We shall get used to it,' said Fancy in the end. 'It's not as if anyone *likes* a lot of noise.'

They fetched the cow out of the wagon, and she slid unsteadily over the cobbles. She mooed and roused a storm of indignant echoes that scattered the gulls perched on the nearby roofs. While Davy led her up to the green Fancy and Harriet saw to the hens, and it was dark before the wagon was unloaded and everything stowed and ship-shape. That night the Garters were too tired to notice that the stars were the only lights out over the bay, or to miss the soft, knocking chorus of fifty boats against the sea wall.

The days that followed were too full to leave much time for brooding. Davy gave up going to sea. Instead, Harriet was sent down the sands each morning with her net to try the pools for shrimps. Davy tended his garden and fished from the harbour wall to catch their dinner. Fancy milked the cow and made butter. She missed the shrimp-boiling less now that she had her churning. She could be heard singing lustily in the little outhouse that she now called the dairy, and she gloated over her pale curls of butter almost as lovingly as she had ladled her rosy shrimps.

At first they all took it for granted that one day, soon, the shrimps would come back. But as the weeks passed and each day, twice a day, the tide came in empty-handed, hope dwindled. So did the Garters' savings. Soon the shrimping season would be over, and the long winter lay ahead, with only a handful of silver to see them through.

After she had gone to bed Harriet would hear Fancy and Davy talking in low worried voices by the dim light of a lamp turned low to save the oil.

Then, one morning, she found out what they had been saying.

'You'll have to go to Aunt Lavinia's, Harriet,' said Fancy. She was in the middle of making bread and was kneading the dough hard.

'We've come down to shells,' she went on, 'though I never thought to live to see the day.'

'But I live here!' cried Harriet. 'I don't want to live with Aunt Lavinia!'

'I didn't say live with her,' said Fancy. 'Just stop with her, and pick up how it's done. Davy and me have the whole thing planned. You stop there with Lavinia and go picking shells—sacks full if you can—to bring back. Then you can learn a few odd tricks, such as threading cockles and such, and home you come. That way, we've a second trade to our hands. If we're lucky, shells will see us through the winter.'

She waved a triumphant, floury hand and Davy nodded from the corner.

'What about my hens?' cried Harriet, looking for a loop-hole. Aunt Lavinia was old, she went in for smelling salts and herb tea and didn't hold with bare feet.

But Harriet knew that she had to go. If she didn't, then *all* the Garters would have to go—perhaps for ever. Secretly, she half wanted to go, once she became used to the idea. Whenever she went to Lower Herring she loved to gather shells, enjoying their dry powdery feel and their bleached colours. Besides, Lower Herring was filled with people, doors stood open and there was talk and laughter. Harriet was tired of echoes and the empty streets of Little Shrimpton.

She packed her bag that evening, taking only the dresses without patches and both her pairs of shoes. Next day, wearing her best blue velvet and two rows of Aunt Lavinia's painted cockles, she went to Lower

Herring, seated between Davy and Fancy on the borrowed farmer's cart.

In Aunt Lavinia's tiny parlour, the walls so thick with shells as to seem barnacled, Davy and Fancy unfolded their plan. Aunt Lavinia nodded frequently and, when they had done, said to Harriet, 'Hold out your hands!'

Puzzled, Harriet spread her fingers.

'Hmm!' said Aunt Lavinia. 'They *might* be good shell fingers. We shall have to see.'

Harriet hid her hands behind her skirts and caught Fancy having a quick look at her own big red fingers before tucking them under the edges of her shawl. Davy did not even bother to look at his, thick and salt-bitten as they were. He just edged them slowly into his pockets and refused a second spiced bun for fear of taking them out again.

It was agreed that Harriet should stay for three weeks.

'Not that she can hope for much in *that* time,' said Aunt Lavinia. 'Hardly time to learn to thread a cockle, let alone oil an oyster or tint a limpet. Sixty years I've been shelling, and even I can sometimes split a scallop or chip a razor clam.'

'Oh, not often, Lavinia, I'm sure,' murmured Fancy.

And Davy jerked his head towards the encrusted walls and said, 'You've a real pretty way with shells, Lavinia, and we're proud to have Harriet learn from you.'

'Oh, well,' said Aunt Lavinia, 'I dare say she *will* learn. And I shall be glad of someone to help with the picking. I don't bend as well as I did.'

'Oh, she can *bend*!' cried Fancy. 'Can't you, Harriet?'

So they all parted cheerfully enough, and as it was only for three weeks there seemed no real need for tears. Harriet shed a few all the same, later, in her new bed with giant whelks for bedknobs and a framed sampler at the head, worked in tiny snails and reading, *Shells are the flowers of the sea.*

'And so are shrimps,' was Harriet's last waking thought as she pulled the stiff sheets over her ears, and all night long tides full of shrimps bloomed for her in dreams.

6

The Sea Piper

When Harriet woke next day she could not at first think where she was. After a few moments she made out the whitish shapes of the whelk bedknobs, and remembered. It was very quiet. There was none of the banging and clatter that Fancy believed in at crack of dawn. Harriet supposed that there was little point in Aunt Lavinia getting up early, as shells could be glued and painted at any time of the day, and picked too, for that matter.

She remembered the sacks she had brought with her to fill with shells and decided to begin straight away. Softly she rose and dressed and tiptoed out, carrying a basket and a pair of shoes. It would never do to come home barefoot. Through the sleeping shell-parlour she stole and out through the back door. A fine white mist blew against her face.

In the distance she could hear the voices of the Lower Herring fishermen as they made their boats ready for the day's sailing. She went in the other direction, out towards the edge of the town where she knew that the sands lay mile upon mile, thickly sown with shells for the gathering. Where the sea wall ended she stopped and buried her shoes under a mound of dry sand. Then she ran down into the mist.

Soon she was picking shells in a white and silent world of her own. Even the sound of the sea was stilled and not a solitary gull called from the hidden town. She might have been at the end of nowhere. On she went, stooping, gathering, seeing how the chalky colours of the shells were brought into life by the dew of mist.

When at last she stopped and straightened up, the mist had begun to lift and was pierced with sun. She saw that she was no longer alone.

The figure she saw might almost have been part of the mist itself, dressed in flowing tatters of grey and blue, thin, spider-legged and swiftly moving. Just then the sun broke through and he stood on stilts of shadow, a sudden giant on the bare, shining flats.

Behind her the gulls began to scream above the town and to race out to sea for their first fish. The figure stopped. He raised a pipe to his lips and began to play. The music was thin and sweet, but crowded, so that it seemed not one melody he played but a thousand, all drawn out of that one slim reed. It had as many voices as the sea itself.

And as he played all the gulls that had flown seaward came winging to him and flew about him, circling and silent. He turned about and stepped away on his steeple legs, still playing, while the gulls followed and Harriet stared herself into a kind of blindness. She did not really see him go at all. One minute he was there, tatters streaming like rags in the mist, the next gone. The music had gone too, and the gulls.

Harriet shaded her eyes and looked back towards the town. The empty roofs glittered in the sun. There was not a gull in sight. Only the weathercock, stone-still with his iron wings, was left.

Harriet picked up her basket of shells and ran, pell-mell, back to the town, fumble-footed in the soft sand. Past the sea wall she flew, up the street and into the kitchen of Aunt Lavinia's house.

'Mercy!' shrieked Aunt Lavinia. 'Where are your shoes, girl?'

They were buried down by the sea wall. Harriet stared at her in her cross-stitched apron, with her frilled cap and ringlets carefully edging her ears.

'I don't *hold* with bare feet,' said Aunt Lavinia.

Harriet knew then, quite certainly, that whatever it was she had seen Aunt Lavinia would not hold with it. Never in a thousand years would she hold with it. She put her basket of shells on the floor and Aunt Lavinia

frowned as little trickles of dry sand ran on to the red tiles.

'I'm sorry,' she said. 'I *did* take my shoes. But I left them buried down by the sea wall.'

'Then *fetch* them!' shrilled Aunt Lavinia. 'Fetch them before the sand gets into the leather!'

Harriet fled.

For the rest of the day she did not leave the house. She dutifully dusted the shells in the parlour and learned how to make glue. She watched Aunt Lavinia turn mussel shells into butter dishes.

But in the evening, after supper, Aunt Lavinia put on her lace mittens, sat in her rocking-chair and nodded off. For the second time that day Harriet stole away and walked the deserted streets of Lower Herring, looking for a gull. The chimney-pots were empty. She *must* have seen what she had seen.

She went back and sorted her shells, waiting for Aunt Lavinia to wake up and go to bed. All the while she thought of the piper leading a ribbon of gulls into nowhere, and wondered.

7

Matthew's Tale

Next day the people of Lower Herring began to notice that the gulls were missing. Harriet went down to the market to fetch a crab for dinner, and everywhere was talk and excitement. To Harriet, who knew exactly what had happened to the gulls, it was odd to hear them guessing.

It was odd, too, to see again so many of her old friends from Lower Shrimpton. They greeted her kindly and asked after Davy and Fancy, but they did not seem happy. 'No sign of the shrimps yet?' they asked wistfully, and Harriet knew that at the first sign of a shrimp's whisker in Shrimpton Bay they would be up on their wagons and bowling helter-skelter back up the coast to home.

Horn she found glumly tarring beams by the pier. There was no carrying for him now, and his horse and cart stood idly by. The hands that had counted silver daily were blackened with pitch, and Harriet wondered if now perhaps he thought shrimps *might* be real fish after all.

The real excitement of the day came in the evening,

when the Lower Herring fleet sailed in. A meeting was held in the square to deal with the matter of the missing sea-gulls. Aunt Lavinia would not go herself for fear of being jostled, but she sent Harriet, bidding her mark well everything that was said.

In the square the Mayor was standing on the stone steps of the market cross, and by his side was a grey-bearded fisherman, bent and leaning on a stick.

'The gulls have flown,' announced the Mayor, waving a pudgy hand towards the sky. 'The shrimps have gone from Little Shrimpton. There's the oddest things going on along this coast, and no one to tell the why or wherefore. It's my opinion that it's the weather that's to blame.'

The crowd muttered and peered up at the sky, looking for signs.

'Old Matthew here,' went on the Mayor, 'thinks *he* knows the answer. I have decided to let him speak.'

The people cheered. Matthew raised his knobbed stick and silence fell.

'It's my belief,' he said, 'that all this is the work of the Sea Piper.'

At his words the hush deepened, not a stir or sound came from the listening people.

'You'll have heard of him, maybe,' Matthew went on. 'You'll have heard tales of him at your mother's knee, how he's the brother of the Pied Piper that brought the rats out of Hamelin and led the children into the mountain. The Sea Piper can lead every living creature of the sea by the notes of his magic pipe. He comes and goes and never a human soul sets eyes on him.'

The Mayor coughed and fidgeted with his chain, but every face in the crowd was turned on the wrinkled, leather-faced fisherman.

'Only a child may see him,' said Matthew, 'and that rarely, once or twice in a hundred years. *I* saw him, eighty years ago and more, and never a word of it have I said until this day.'

A soft gasp ran about the square and ebbed away.

'I saw him on yon very beach,' said Matthew, 'piping

sea-gulls to him in a mist. I asked him why he stole our gulls, and he said, for loneliness. "I pipe alone with my own shadow," says he. "Always alone. That is why I take the gulls. But I shall bring them back before long." And sure enough he did, that very night. Out of the whole town there was only me to know they had gone at all. They came at sunset.' He looked beyond to the darkening sky over the sea. 'At about the time of day it is now. I saw them fly back over the chimney-pots and ran down that road, down that beach, as fast as the wind. But he was gone.'

Harriet, her heart thudding, looked up at the empty chimney-pots and the silvery streaked sky, and all in a moment knew what she must do. No one saw her leave the square or heard her flying footsteps over the cobbled road down to the sea.

As she started down the long empty beach, away from the town, beyond the gasping of her own breath Harriet thought she heard the sea-gulls. She stopped for a minute, listening. Very faint and far away she heard them, and though she strained her eyes into the gloom she could see no sign of them. She saw only the faint fringe of sea glowing in the darkness, and the last silvery shreds of daylight in the sky.

She ran again along the firmer sand newly left by the tide. The wet sand closed her footprints behind her.

She left no trace. And all the while the crying of gulls grew louder until suddenly they went over in a rain of white. Their crying deafened her and she did not hear the Sea Piper's music until she saw him, face to face.

She stopped. He stood a little way from her, still piping. His tatters seemed one with the darkness as they had with the mist, and she could make out only the pale shape of his face. The gulls' cries faded, the music died away and he took the pipe from his lips. He did not speak, and for fear that he had not seen her and would be gone in an instant with his quick light strides as he had that morning, Harriet called softly, 'Sea Piper! Sea Piper!'

He nodded slowly.

'Sea Piper, help us, please!'

She thought he bent his head as if ready to listen, and she poured out the story of how first the shrimps had gone from Little Shrimpton, and now the people themselves, leaving only the Garters and their echoes. She told how the weeds were growing between the stones and the birds nesting in the deserted houses.

'And soon *we* shall have to go, too!' she cried desperately. 'We can't stay for ever without shrimps, even *Fancy* says that!'

The Sea Piper was slowly nodding and Harriet thought that he smiled.

'And, Sea Piper,' she said then, remembering old Matthew's words, 'we will make you a gift in return. You shall have all the gulls of Little Shrimpton, every one of them. You shall pipe them away and keep them for ever, for company on your journeys.'

She stood silent. In the distance came voices and shouting. The people of Lower Herring had seen the gulls fly home and were hurrying to the beach in the hope of a glimpse of the Sea Piper.

'Oh, quickly, quickly!' cried Harriet. 'Please give me your answer.'

He nodded suddenly. 'I will do it,' he said. 'And now listen, what you must do.'

Harriet listened eagerly while all the time the shouting grew louder, and just as the light of torches fell on to them and the Sea Piper's shadow sprang to a steeple again, he had done and was gone.

The dark swallowed him at a single gulp as the mist had done.

Harriet turned to face the bobbing army of torches, blinking at the dazzle.

'Why, it's Harriet Garter!' she heard the Shrimpton people cry, and 'Who is it? Who is it?' from the Lower Herring folk, who did not know her face.

'Have you seen him? Did you see him?' the cry went up then from all alike, and Harriet smiled.

'I have seen him and I have spoken with him,' she replied, 'and I asked him a favour, which he has granted. All the people of Little Shrimpton must be home by tomorrow night, because, the day after, the men will have to be up early. The shrimps will be back in the bay.'

There was a moment's silence and then a roar went up, rocking the torchlight and sending shadows swinging far out over the sands. All of a sudden Harriet found herself being lifted and carried shoulder high, with the heads of the procession bobbing below her. The noise and light left the beach and went up into the town. Only the Sea Piper walked the shore alone, hugging the promise of a hundred gulls and the end of silence.

8

Piping up the Shrimps

At dawn next day Harriet was packing her bag while Aunt Lavinia slumbered on, worn out by the goings-on of the night before. When Harriet had been borne home by the excited townspeople, treading on her garden and waving torches in her dazzled eyes, Aunt Lavinia had needed her smelling-salts immediately. When she came round after the first sniff to see so many faces bending over her she had gone straight off again, and Harriet had felt obliged to show the visitors out.

Aunt Lavinia had not believed a word of the story about the Sea Piper and was inclined to think that the gulls had not really disappeared at all. As for the rest of it, it was simply a trick of Harriet's to get herself home again.

'*I* never heard of shrimps dancing along to pipes,' she said. 'Nobody *I* ever knew played tunes for the fishes.'

'Of course not!' cried Harriet. 'But this is magic!'

'I don't *hold* with magic,' retorted Aunt Lavinia, and went to bed.

Harriet knew it was unlikely that Aunt Lavinia had changed in the night and would wake up believing in magic with all her heart, so she tiptoed out as she had done that first morning, barefoot and carrying her bag. The sack of shells she left behind with a little paper saying goodbye and thank you. Aunt Lavinia had meant no harm. She simply could not help being Aunt Lavinia.

The Little Shrimpton folk were already gathering in the square. They had worked through the night so as to be ready for the journey home. And the rattling of the wagons and their hoarse, excited talk woke the rest of the town, so that soon the streets were as crowded as if it were noon and not still starlight—except at the very eastern edge of the sky.

By the time the whole procession had gathered and the first carts began to trundle out of the square, it was daylight. Harriet, perched on a wagon with a friendly shrimper and his family, almost choked with excitement. And when at last in the afternoon the cart began the long roll down the hill into Little Shrimpton itself, and Harriet saw Davy and Fancy come running out to stare huge-eyed at the advancing wagons, she burst into tears, as she had been tempted to do for most of the day.

Then it was all cheering and shouting, shaking of

hands, clapping of backs, and such joy on the faces of Fancy and Davy that you would have thought the heavens had opened and begun to *rain* shrimps.

All Harriet could say was, 'The shrimps are coming back! The shrimps are coming back!' And it was only later, when they were inside and Harriet was sitting on the new chair Davy had carved for her, that she told them the whole story.

This time she had a real audience for her tale. There were plenty of things that Fancy herself did not hold with, but magic was definitely not one of them. She gasped and exclaimed extravagantly all through the telling, and at the end said, 'Well! The *Sea Piper*! Would he come in and have a bite of supper, after, do you think?'

Then Harriet told them what the Sea Piper had made her promise. At sunset, the moment the first star appeared, everyone in Little Shrimpton was to go inside and close the doors and shutters. If so much as a chink showed behind a curtain, he would not keep his promise. No one, not even Harriet herself, was to set eyes on him while the spell was worked.

Fancy was thoroughly disappointed.

'And from what you say, Harriet, he could have done with a good meal,' she said wistfully. And Davy added, 'I should have liked to shake him by the hand, and so, I dare say, would every man in Little Shrimpton.'

The day passed quickly. Doors and windows were thrown wide, mats were beaten and dust flew in clouds. By the time evening came every family in Shrimpton was sitting down to supper in its own home, and the Garters themselves felt that theirs was a real home once more, now that the people were back.

'I dare say we shall miss the gulls a bit at first,' said Fancy, 'but not so much as we missed people. Oh no! And I don't begrudge that poor Piper his bit of company, either.'

As the sun began to set a wind blew up from the sea, rattling the doors and windows as if to remind the villagers of their part of the bargain. And so, one by one, with a last look at the sky and sea, each family went indoors.

One by one the shutters came across and very soon the Garters were in a street as dark and silent as it had been for the past months, only this time there was a difference. They knew that the lamps were burning, even if they were not seen, and the voices there, even though they could not be heard.

The wind blew stronger with every moment, tossing Harriet's skirts about her knees and sending Fancy's hands flying to her hair.

'Come along now,' said Davy. 'Inside.'

He guessed that the two of them were loitering,

half hoping for a glimpse of the Piper, despite everything.

'A promise is a promise, Fancy and Harriet,' he said.

As they turned to come in, the gulls that had been settling to roost on the roofs and chimney-pots suddenly flew up and began to scream anew, riding on the wind, treading the great gusts as if they were waves at sea.

'He's coming!' shrieked Fancy, suddenly overcome by the thought of magic about to happen on her doorstep. Next minute the Garters were inside and the doors and shutters banged shut.

They waited then, and listened.

At first they heard only the wind, thundering and buffeting about the walls until the little house trembled and the oil-lamps flickered in the cross-draughts. Above the wind they heard the endless crying of the gulls and at last, thin and high, threading the tumult as clearly as a bell, the music of the Sea Piper.

The Garters sat heads cocked, spellbound.

'Is he calling the shrimps, d'you think, or the sea-gulls?' whispered Fancy.

'The shrimps,' said Harriet softly.

She could see them in her mind's eye, wreathing the bay in their shadowy thousands, pulled by the notes promising whatever delights a shrimp dreams of, longs for in his shrimpmost heart.

For a moment the piping stopped. Then came a new

music, one that Harriet half remembered. The gulls renewed their screaming, and she pictured the Sea Piper striding off now with his catch of white birds, tatters flowing like water behind him in the wind, long legs stepping lightly into nowhere.

The music grew fainter, the last gulls' cries were drowned in the wind. Last of all, the wind dropped, the wooden house steadied itself and stood firm again. The Sea Piper had passed.

Fancy drew a vast, shuddering sigh that was like the last breath of the wind itself.

'Oh, Davy!' she said softly. 'Oh, Harriet! It was magic! Perfect magic!'

The others nodded slowly.

'And now,' she said, with some of her old briskness, 'what about your oilskins for the morning, Davy? And where did you leave your net, Harriet? You'll be shrimping tomorrow, I'll be bound.'

And so she was. At first light Harriet was running down the puddled sands, woken by her own excitement, for there was not a gull left in sight. As she reached her first pool she stopped only for a moment to wave an arm to Davy, outward bound.

Then she looked down into the clear depths to see shrimps at last and, for a brief moment before she broke the water with her net, a ragged shape that might have been the reflection of a cloud—or of the Sea Piper?

STAY ON

Here are details of other exciting TARGET titles. If you cannot obtain these books from your local bookshop, or newsagent, write to the address below listing the titles you would like and enclosing cheque or postal order—*not* currency—including 7p per book to cover packing and postage; 2–4 books, 5p per copy; 5–8 books, 4p per copy.

TARGET BOOKS,
Universal-Tandem Publishing Co.,
14 Gloucester Road,
London SW7 4RD

THE POND ON MY WINDOW-SILL 30p
Christopher Reynolds
0 426 10057 3
The companion volume to SMALL CREATURES IN MY BACK GARDEN. The author tells you how to establish an indoor aquarium with snails, tadpoles, water-beetles and other tiny creatures easily obtainable from nearby pond or stream. A fascinating and instructive hobby for all ages. *Illustrated.*

PETER PIPPIN'S SECOND BOOK OF PUZZLES 25p
0 426 10102 2
Thousands of young people all over the country tackle Peter Pippin's puzzles every week in their local paper. Here is another collection to baffle and entertain the whole family!

If you enjoyed this book and would like to have information sent you about other TARGET titles, write to the address below.

You will also receive:
A FREE TARGET BADGE!
Based on the TARGET BOOKS symbol—see front cover of this book—this attractive three-colour badge, pinned to your blazer-lapel or jumper, will excite the interest and comment of all your friends!

and you will be further entitled to:
FREE ENTRY INTO THE TARGET DRAW!
All you have to do is cut off the coupon beneath, write on it your name and address in *block capitals*, and pin it to your letter. Twice a year, in June and December, coupons will be drawn 'from the hat' and the winner will receive a complete year's set of TARGET books.

Write to:

TARGET BOOKS,
Universal-Tandem
Publishing Co.
14, Gloucester Road,
London SW7 4RD

If you live in New Zealand, write to:

TARGET BOOKS,
Whitcoulls Ltd.,
111, Cashel Street,
Christchurch

If you live in South Africa, write to:

TARGET BOOKS,
Purnell & Sons,
505, C.N.A. Building,
110, Commissioner Street,
Johannesburg

If you live in Australia, write to:

TARGET BOOKS,
Rical Enterprises Pty. Ltd.,
Daking House,
11, Rawson Place,
Sydney, N.S. Wales 2000

———————— cut here ————————

Full name..

Address..

....

....

Age..................................

PLEASE ENCLOSE A SELF-ADDRESSED ENVELOPE WITH YOUR COUPON.